Penguin Books
THE PENGUIN BOOK
OF AUSTRALIAN WOMEN

Susan Hampton was born in Inverell, New South Wales, in 1949. Previous publications include *Sister Poets 1* (Sisters Publishing, 1979), *Costumes* (Transit Press, 1981) and *About Literature* with Sue Woolfe (Macmillan, 1984). Her poems and stories have been published in many Australian magazines and anthologies, and in 1979 she won the Dame Mary Gilmore Award. She received writing grants from the Literature Board in 1979, 1983 and 1984. Susan Hampton has a B.A. (Hons) in English and currently teaches writing courses at Newcastle CAE and the New South Wales Institute of Technology in Sydney. She is a single parent and has one son.

Kate Llewellyn was born at Tumby Bay, South Australia, in 1940. Previous publications include *Sister Poets 1* (Sisters Publishing, 1979), *Trader Kate and the Elephants* (Friendly Street Poets, 1982) and *Luxury* (Redress Press, 1985), and her poems and stories have been included in a number of anthologies. She received writing grants from the Literature Board of the Australia Council in 1982 and 1984, and in 1982 was the joint winner of the Anne Elder Award. She has a B.A. in History and Classics and has worked as a registered nurse and a joint owner/director of an art gallery. Kate Llewellyn has a son and a daughter. She now writes full-time and lives in Leura in the Blue Mountains.

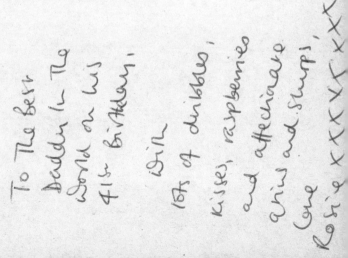

THE PENGUIN BOOK OF
AUSTRALIAN WOMEN POETS

edited by Susan Hampton and Kate Llewellyn

PENGUIN BOOKS

Published with the assistance of the
Literature Board of the Australia Council

Penguin Books Australia Ltd,
487 Maroondah Highway, PO Box 257
Ringwood, Victoria 3134, Australia
Penguin Books Ltd,
Harmondsworth, Middlesex, England
Penguin Books,
40 West 23rd Street, New York, NY 10010, USA
Penguin Books Canada Limited,
2801 John Street, Markham, Ontario, Canada L3R 1B4
Penguin Books (NZ) Ltd,
182-190 Wairau Road, Auckland 10, New Zealand

First published by Penguin Books Australia, 1986

Typset in California by Midland Typesetters, Maryborough
Made and printed in Australia by The Dominion Press-Hedges & Bell

CIP

The Penguin book of Australian women poets.

Includes index.
ISBN 0 14 058575 3 (pbk.).

1. Australian poetry—Women authors. I. Hampton, Susan,
1949-   . II. Llewellyn, Kate, 1940-

A821'.008'09287

For our mothers, June Mackie and Tommy Brinkworth

CONTENTS

EDITORS' NOTE

We'd like to thank the Literature Board of the Australia Council for research funding for this project. In particular we thank Anna Ward, Tom Shapcott, Irene Stevens and Elaine Lindsay for their help.

Special thanks to Jocelyn Stenson for her love, support and help with the work; to Robert Stead, for his help; and to Clare O'Brien, our editor at Penguin, for her understanding and patience.

We also thank the following people for comments and work on the Introduction, for help with research and work in libraries, for reading the manuscript, lending books, providing legal advice, and for their hospitality: Catherine Berndt, Lisa Berryman, Baiba Berzins, Colleen Burke, Foyle Campbell, Alison Clark, Brigid Costello, Anna Couani, Liz Day, Sarah Day, Tamsin Donaldson, Marianne Erhart, Chris Fondum, Barbara Giles, Heather Grey, Sylvia Hale, Beni Hampton, Nancy Harding, Beth Haynes, Rob Johnson, Sylvia Kantaris, Jacquie Kent, Nancy Keesing, Margaret Kibble, George Kosovich, Guida Lawrence, Caroline Llewellyn, Kathleen Mackie, Trisha Mackie, Chris Mansell, Billy Marshall-Stoneking, Philip Martin, Andrew McDonald, Violet McLean, Gina Mercer, Max Meyer, Drusilla Modjeska, Dao Nguyen, Margaret O'Hagan, Kim Paul, Gerry Rogers, Judith Rodriguez, Gig Ryan, Mary Savage Harrison, Howard Schrieber, Susan Sheridan, Tina Slon, Lynne Spender, Amanda Stenson, Jono Stenson, Amanda Stewart, Christine Squires, Bobbi Sykes, Frank Thompson, John Tranter, Jim Tulip, Anthony Wallace, Elizabeth Webby, Jennifer Wilson, Sue Woolfe and Merril Yule.

INTRODUCTION

Here are eighty-nine women poets. Tribal Aboriginal singers through to post-modern writers and performance poets of 1986. This collection is part of a history of women's writing and of cultural politics which are creatively disturbing the conventional view of our literary heritage. The selection charts the possibilities of women's writing. It also presents for the first time an overview of the traditions, the voices and the range of women's poetry in Australia.

poems which know why

We looked for poems which gave us a shock of recognition, which gave pleasure. Which acknowledge female experience. We looked for poems which redescribe traditional themes like sex and motherhood, and also for poems on 'unfeminine' subjects. Poems which look at feminity as a cultural construct, and how we live inside it. Or outside it. We looked for poems which have an awareness of their form, of the processes of consciousness and of writing. Poems which are aware of the link between formal experimentation and gender. Poems which know why and the language itself knows. We looked for surprises.

Rhymed verse is a wide net through which many subtleties escape. Nor would I take it to capture a strong thing, such as a whale.

Anna Wickham, born 1884
from 'Note on Rhyme'

Our perspective is feminist, but the-feminist-poet has become a stereotype. And there are many feminisms. For us and many poets in this book, the women's movement has created a network of friendships and ideas, a politics from which we can understand the culture, and a knowledge of each other's writing. A dialogue which we're echoing off each other becomes a new dialectic.

I have been most influenced by writing done by women. Their experience was the same as mine. Both the migrant and the woman are in the same position. They have to deal with conflict. The migrant is placed outside the norms of society. The woman has to establish an identity for herself other than the one she is offered. As both a woman and a migrant I have been given no sense of belonging in the

world, no set place. I have to state my identity. I have to reconstruct the world.
My writing deals with stress, chaos, and the need to express this and thus reconstruct
my world, through the record of my personal experience. This way I make my own
experience coherent. I join me to the world.[1]

Ania Walwicz

15 well-known collections

In fifteen well-known collections of Australian poetry published since 1970,
the average of female authors selected was 17 per cent. The average number
of pages of women's poetry was 13 per cent.[2] This may not be a problem
of deliberate critical neglect, but a problem of consciousness — until recently
most anthology editors, literary historians and critics have been male, and
their gaze was unconsciously focussed on other men. What is represented,
why certain discourses are approved, is always in question. Which books
get published and reviewed, and why? Which poets are taught in high
schools, universities, teachers' colleges? These are all areas where feminists
are challenging established attitudes and discourses.

I believe creating (writing poetry in this case) should be, and is, as natural and
integrated a process as cooking eggs for breakfast; can see no distinction between
a person wishing to express herself on the page, or getting drunk and attempting
to communicate verbally in a pub. Each moment, each experience is unique, as
therefore each poem is . . . If a poem is emotional, subjective, hysterical even, then
chances are the form will be scattered over the page as randomly as the emotions
which motivate it. I want a poetry of the spirit/of the body/ of the emotions.[3]

Vicki Viidikas, 1973

Women's poems have been criticised at times for being too subjective,
too personal, too 'domestic'. Critical language has a repertoire of syntax,
adjectives and metaphors for casting its own light on reality. 'Academic
objectivity' goes on revealing itself as the ideology of conservatism.[4]

> . . . and think
> of my men friends who criticise
> my writing for being too personal
> whatever that means
> ah I know
> and ever since I can remember I
> strove to be depersonalised — did you?
>
> . . . I still have my role
> my invisibility
> but changed older different
> I am uneasy
> in these close fitting garments

Colleen Burke
from 'Call Around and See Us'

reconstructing the world means rethinking

Women have a marginal status in the literary world, otherwise this book would not be necessary. Having to reconstruct the world means rethinking. The power of the margins is exactly in the reconstruction. There is a way of understanding the centre from the margins.

In reply to the interview question 'What is the voice of your poetry?' Jennifer Maiden said in 1977:

Ambivalent, ambidextrous, ambiguous, androgynous, amorous, ironic . . . I see my work as inviting my reader to wander in it and explore without having his way barred by any immediate and dismissive simplicity in the poem's voice. Teasing, intellectual irony, too, has always seemed to me a humane new channel toward pensive seduction for what otherwise, in more direct poetry, can be a jealous urge for power over the reader.

My work, however, is as much concerned with science as sensuality, and with political and ontological theory as much as with the domestic solidities. Technically, I like poetry to be rich and inexhaustible, but I am prepared to use brevity and obviousness when they are useful to a thought-process or to stylistic effect.[5]

Whether discussing formal techniques or subject matter, women writers often speak about dichotomies, making distinctions. We also write about breaking distinctions, especially those in the forms of writing—blurring the line between poetry and prose, or fiction and criticism. Breaking the old forms, multiplying the meanings, inviting new juxtapositions.

Writing *A Gap in the Records*,[6] a post-modern spy thriller, Jan McKemmish said she wanted to put *women* and *power* in the same sentence. Reviewers now find themselves putting *feminist* and *spy thriller* in the same sentence.

The margins are becoming visible. It's not just that large numbers of women are now writing the other half of the story—what it felt like to be Rapunzel or Mrs Noah, though that is important too: the rewriting of mythical and legendary female figures is one visible pattern in this book. Woven under the surfaces of these poems is the consciousness of a new sort of woman, and this changes the way we write.

Experimentation with form is an absolute necessity for a woman writer. For what has been done and how that was done neither says what she has to say nor provides the way of saying it.[7]

Finola Moorhead, 1985

Could be as limiting as a slavish worship of traditionalism.

I have to state my identity

We tend to think of a powerful man as a born leader and a powerful woman as an anomaly.

Margaret Atwood

It all started when I engaged in a very feminine pursuit — I persuaded my husband that we should learn round-dancing. For the benefit of uninitiated readers I will explain that round-dancing is an up-to-date version of old-fashioned dances such as the Pride of Erin and the Canadian three-step.

Each dance has an intricate series of patterned movements that go with a specific piece of music. To learn these, the couples stand in a circle, so that all move in the same direction, while someone calls out the movements.

The calls are all directed to the men, who are leading the women, as is usual in dancing. Thus a caller will say: 'Two forward two-steps, walk two, and face the wall.' This means that the man does two forward two-steps, walks two steps forward, and then turns sideways to face the wall. But the woman does two backward two-steps, walks two steps backward, and turns away from the wall. She thus has to do a kind of simultaneous translation, and therefore makes mistakes far more often than the man.

I took all this for granted, of course, until we reached a dance where there were a lot of instructions to do backward two-steps and backward walks. For the first time the women seemed to be going forwards most of the time, though, of course, we were being instructed to go backwards. I discovered that this was my favourite dance, and also that my husband did not like it at all.

For some time we did not realise why, until it hit me that all my life I had been dancing mostly backwards while he had been going forwards. When you dance backwards, you can't see where you are going and so you have no control over whether you might bump into someone — you are in someone else's hands.

I noticed that when our roles were suddenly reversed for one dance, my husband felt totally insecure.

This story encapsulates for me the problems inherent in a sexist society. Let me emphasise that I was quite happy dancing backwards and doing simultaneous translations. It was not until I had the experience of walking forwards for the first time — and of repeating that experience a number of times — that I even became aware that not everyone spent their life walking backwards and that there was an alternative which was much nicer.

As an acknowledged anti-sexist, I don't want to reverse the whole process and have men walk backwards, translating, all their lives. What I want is a society in which each half of the population gets a turn at speaking the main language, at learning the subordinate one, and at walking — and dancing — in both directions.[8]

Erica Bates, 1984

I have to state my identity. I have to reconstruct the world . . . this way I make my own experience coherent. I join me to the world.

Ania Walwicz

These could all be read as statements representing possible layers in the evolution of a feminist consciousness. The Margaret Atwood quote is an example of the cryptic sentence which triggers the first stage — we realise the strength of the codes of behaviour which pattern our thinking, and how hard it is to change. We observe our relationships with men, our roles in the fluent dance of patriarchy. Behaviour we had taken for granted is now in question. Our statements are threatening to anyone who wants to preserve inequality, and particularly anyone afflicted with machismo. ('A bruised machismo is not the same as a broken head. It's worse.' — Angela Carter.)

A radical questioning of social structures often leads to an angry stage, chaos, which makes way for a new layer, creation. Making something new is to imagine different grids on reality, other views of the world.

maps for the future

The map of the world is felt from the inside. Rough around the coastlines and smooth over the hills and sand dunes. Warm and moist through the rivers which lead outside to the forests like long hair then sparser like shorter more bristly hair to the touch. Reading a globe of the world with its topography in relief. Reading with the fingers as though blind. Feeling it with the back, down the spine. Making contact with the nipples and the nose only. Moving at a fast rate underwater through the oceans and large lakes. Most of the oceans connect up with each other. Moving so fast that you become aware of the earth's surface being curved. Flying low but fast across the land masses. Make yourself feel like the world. As old but not as troubled.[9]

Anna Couani, 1983

In women writers' workshops, women's studies courses, writers are working out the social meaning of their literary techniques. It has become clear that ideas can't be divorced from the way they are presented.

'Once I look at the formal techniques of the writing, I can tell what is being said.'

'Maybe we should talk about the difference between story language, non-narrative fiction, and writer's notebook language.'

Feminist critical theory has moved from the insights of de Beauvoir, Greer and Millett to the theories of Kristeva, Cixous, Irigary. The -feminist-writer is a stereotype which is constantly being deconstructed by the many available feminisms. In the poems, deliberate formal naivety may go together with highly sophisticated subject matter. Other poems work in a different way against fixed meanings, showing in their new forms a shifting play of self-consciousness.

I'm interested in patterns, mainly their disruption. Poetry should at some level disorganize the world. Language should through new customs declare its baggage, have it inspected and sniffed for details.[10]

Chris Mansell, 1985

Poetry is language in search of itself.[11]
Joanne Burns, 1985

What are the strategies of the new writing? Why does contemporary poetry often call up the response 'It doesn't sound like a poem'?

In the last five years I've been working towards a plainer, more colloquial, clipped short line, a dramatic, uncluttered utterance, with the use of ampersands lower case and a minimum of punctuation to speed up the phrasing. Behind it all is the sound of the human voice talking and the jagged inconsequential nature of thought. I became sick to death of the personal pronoun 'I' and began to write through a persona called Alice. I try to use myth and symbol interrelated with the tough and 'unpoetic' stuff of modern life.[12]

Dorothy Hewett, 1985

Until my late teens my environment was cafes. I witnessed women being bought for a meal (the assertive, well-dressed ones could name their price). It was these women who had the most influence on my life. I started writing poetry in 1972. Poetry armed me, so I began to squeeze pens and write. Seizing the pen and moving words along a production line is like holding the carnival that comes to town in your land.[13]

thalia, 1985

One of the features of modern poetry readings is the performance poem, which includes the idea of the poem 'off the page'. What constitutes a poem may come from what looks like a poem, or prose, or a song, or a musical score. Syntactical disruptions, discontinuity, truncations, bizarre serial imagery, repetition, are some of the strategies of this sort of poem, and can be seen here in the work of such writers as Gig Ryan, Ania Walwicz, Amanda Stewart. The influence of dadaism, and particularly of Gertrude Stein ('the mama of dada') is seen in the undoing of known forms, in the use of language that is clearly against the 'machine drive' of the late twentieth century, and is opposed to the push to a future based on the fetish of technology.

Another field of contemporary poetry which should be mentioned here is that area where poetry, criticism and poetics overlap. Traditional genres are called into question by formal playfulness. At times the poem takes as its subject the nature of the relationship between poet, poem and reader.

> . . . Don't trust
> me yet: I don't know what I will still
> require of you, and you don't know
> as yet the depth and danger in your trust.
> There is no room here to run, and none
> in you that I can run from.
>
> Jennifer Maiden
> from 'The Trust'

the last twenty years

We know about the changes in Australian poetry that came in the late 1960s with the influence of American poetry and the subculture which produced sex-drugs-and-rock-'n'-roll as its slogan. Rock-'n'-roll was mainly about men but there is a continuous tradition of women from Janis Joplin to Patti Smith to Laurie Anderson — and their influence can be heard in some of the poems here. In the late 1960s the poetic voice became colloquial and political. It was no longer hip to be warlike. Modern anthologies have caught up with this.

In the 1970s, feminism affected many women in a personal and direct way. It changed our lives. At the same time, men were being politicised by the anti-Vietnam war movement. For women the two overlapped — the women's peace movement has been active in Australia from World War I to Pine Gap, and the influence of peace thinking, peace songs, can be heard in some poems. Along with the feminist critiques of militarism, the issues of sexism and racism were discussed.

As a body of ideas, feminism has absorbed the 60s ethos of collective action, the notions of being anti-star and anti-authoritarian. Because it addresses the equality of women it automatically brings up the equality of people.

Anna Couani

Thinking we had no voice in history, we began consciously looking for a tradition of women's writing. We realised there had to be more than what was represented in official histories. Research for this anthology showed a suppressed tradition of left and feminist writing in Australia.

In the same way, the major influence of feminist ideas on the poetry of the 1970s has not been recorded in current anthologies. Our record exists in *Mother I'm Rooted*, edited by Kate Jennings and published in 1975.

It was a collection of voices, many unknown, of women writing in the early 1970s. In mainstream literary circles, it was generally thought to be embarrassing. It was meant to be. It was meant to be said. And some of it was the best thing that had happened to modern women's writing in Australia. Outback Press printed 4000 copies and they sold out. In Australia this is big sales for a book of poetry. All over the country women who had been accustomed to seeing themselves as inhabitants in men's poems, (*La Belle Dame*, etc.) were hearing from themselves.

The book provoked a debate about standards, invited both by the poetry and Kate Jennings' introduction.

> Some poems fall anyhow,
> all of a heap anywhere, dishevelled,
> legs apart in loneliness and
> desperation,
> and you talk about standards
>
> Sylvia Kantaris
> from 'By their poems ye shall know them: poem'

I don't know any longer what is 'good' and what is 'bad'. I have been trained to know, in a patriarchal university, on a diet of male writers. We have to go back to bedrock, and explore thoroughly that which is female and that which is male, and then perhaps we can approach androgyny, and humanity.

Kate Jennings

Most critics ignored the book. Women writers couldn't afford to ignore it, after all, here we were, talking. When Finola Moorhead reviewed the book she was mapping the future.

There is a peculiar mixing of old-fashioned styles with crude innovations in the techniques occurring throughout the book – a polarity which suggests that this is the first step towards a new feminine poetic genre. The first step being to do, to be honest and to risk failure. The next step will be to look into the failures and successes, and then to risk failure again by reaching out from the successes towards a satisfactory form which will be able to express the deep changes women are experiencing, the inventive thought and reassessment of basic principles that these changes demand.[14]

In 1977 the Poets Union was formed. It is active in organising readings, seminars, bookstalls, etc. Many of the women involved are feminists, and it is now Poets Union policy to present the same numbers of women readers as men. The network of readers, which has been essential for some of the poets in this anthology, has called into question the old ideas about poets. One is the dominant image of the poet as male; another is that a writer works best alone in a garret, separated from his or her peers by a burning

sense of duty to Art. Links were created between singers, artists and poets
with an ideological commitment to validating the work of women, migrants
and writers who did not fit the established notions of poetic practice.

The latest changes affecting Australian poetry came with French-
influenced New York poetry, and the writing practices of post-modernism.
Semiotic theory, structuralism and the techniques of deconstruction have
had an enormous effect on contemporary experimental writing. Feminism
absorbs ideas for developing other interpretations of reality and builds on
them so that the theories also confront racism and sexism. All the time
we are exploring the notion of what power is. A colleague has said:

It's possible that post-modernism will be seen as a baroque manifestation and
women's writing as the major movement of the late twentieth century.

notes for a feminist history

In the last ten years, there has been an upsurge of women writer's
workshops, women's studies courses, and feminist magazines. There are
also visible changes in small press publishing and editing.

Some feminist presses — Sisters Publishing, McPhee Gribble, Redress
Press, Sybylla, No Regrets, TuTu Press, Tantrum Press, Sea Cruise, Pariah
Press, Abalone Press. Some small presses have chosen to publish women
equally with men, including Friendly Street, Transit and Black Lightning.

Other small presses, distributors and magazines where women have been
influential — Saturday Club, Power Press, Rigmarole Books, Allbooks,
Collected Works Bookshop, Murphy Sisters, the Feminist Bookshop, Shrew
Bookshop, *Tabloid Story*, *925*, *Migrant 7* and *Brave New World*.

Some feminist writers have taken up the stance of self-publishing as a
positive alternative to the way things work in the publishing world — among
them Peg Clarke, Mary Fallon, Pam Brown.

Some women editors of academic literary journals, little magazines, and
feminist journals include Cheryl Adamson *New Poetry*, Fay Zwicky
Westerly, Judith Rodriguez and Judith Brett *Meanjin*, Grace Perry *Poetry
Australia*, Pat Laird *SCOPP*, Susan Higgins *Southern Review*, Cheryl Frost
Linq, Helen Weller *Artlook*, Chris Mansell, Dorothy Porter and Joanne
Burns *Compass*, Wendy Morgan and Sneja Gunew *Mattoid*, Barbara Giles
Luna, Carole Ferrier *Hecate*, Jurate Sasnaitis and Berni Janssen *Syllable*.

Many magazines which are specifically feminist are edited by
collectives — *Refractory Girl*, *Womanspeak*, *Scarlet Women*, *Lip*, *Come*

2, *Skirt*, *Girls Own*. Many more have come and gone, archives of women's history, politics and poetry, such as *Mejane* and *Mabel*.[15]

There have been women journal editors for a long time. From 1884 to 1894 Mary Hannay Foott was the literary editor of the *Queenslander*. Louisa Lawson, a pioneer of women's suffrage and feminism generally, founded and edited the *Dawn*, a women's newspaper. Mary Gilmore edited a widely read women's page in the Sydney *Worker* for twenty-three years. Bessie Mitchell (Guthrie) set up the feminist Viking Press in the 1940s.

back to the beginning

It is a long way from the shifting definitions and values which mark our age to the origins of Australian poetry. Poetry has been sung and danced and chanted here for many thousands of years. There are some older Aborigines who carry around in their memories the words to several thousand 'verses' of songs.

The land is full of stories, no matter where you look. That tree is really a digging stick left by a giant woman; and that rock over there is a dingo's nose; and that cave is where the finch women escaped the anger of marapulpa, the spider . . . The old storytellers say, 'the dreaming does not end; it is not like the whitefellas' way. What happened once, happens again and again. This is the power of the Song. Through the singing,' they say, 'we keep everything alive.'[16]

Billy Marshall-Stoneking

We begin this anthology with extracts — in the original language and in translation — from Aboriginal women's songs, but finding them was a difficult and paradoxical research task. Until the last twenty years or so, most anthropologists have been men, and they spoke mainly to male Aborigines and collected their songs. Compared with the large body of research done on 'men's business', very little is available, particularly song texts, which reflects women's view of the world. About the women in the background, suppositions were made, sometimes wildly incorrect. It would be easy to get the impression that women sang only grief and fertility songs, but more women anthropologists and linguists are now working with Aboriginal women and studying their songs. Some of this material is secret; very little is yet available in a form which can be 'read' as a poem.

To begin with, the songs are not (in our sense) 'poems', and were never meant to go anywhere near a page. Then too, some performances are for women only, some for men only and in others, women and men join with different roles. A performance has a spectacle aspect (song, mime, dance, body paint) which is not conveyed by print. Things which on the page impress by their economy, in performance impress by their patterned repetition, their 'prolongability'.[17]

There are issues of transmission, such as: Did a woman invent this song? and: Is this secret, or can we 'take' it? We might find that another person or tribal group owns the song, and that the singer has been given permission to sing it, sometimes with local variations. In some cases the song was given to the owner in a dream. Is the author the person, animal or being in the dream?

Non-Aboriginal Australians are interested in authorship and composition because we live in a culture of the printed word, whereas Aborigines are interested in ownership and performance.

If we take it that the 'author' is the owner of the song, we're still faced with the problem of the song being filtered through the values of the translator. Then there is the literary tradition to contend with. In the past, some translators thought part of their job was to 'dignify' the Aboriginal song by making references and comparisons to the classical European canon and to Greek and Roman mythology. It makes a bizarre impression to see an Aboriginal song conveyed into Victorian rhymed verse.

Another problem confronting the translator of traditional songs is that many songs have several layers of meaning. We came across a literal translation of a sequence of song words which in English read

    sunset   sunset   sunset   sunset

and it was explained that there were four different ways of talking about the sunset and its meaning in the song.

A text may contain words which aren't used in ordinary speech, but are 'power' words, as they are described in some languages. The Aboriginal languages have oblique ways of referring to all sorts of principles and powers — these are 'in the beginning was the word' words. Further, there are grades of initiation into the meaning of things. In an oral culture which is close-knit, a high degree of allusion is possible and valued. Sometimes the allusion is a way of restricting access to privileged knowledge.[18]

Maureen Watson, black activist and story-teller, has said that

For a people who now call themselves Australian, and call our country their country, both teachers and students have remarkably little knowledge or respect for the rich cultural heritage and tradition of the land with which they identify so, so strongly.[19]

quiet

It's quiet in the social studies lesson. She is colouring in a picture of some men and horses and a mountain. The whisper starts, and she thinks it's the wind in the trees she is putting on the mountain. But no, it's the women talking, where are they? On the first page of her book is a picture, blue and red and white, of Captain Cook. On the second page some women are getting off a ship. Then two men in a little boat going towards the bottom of the map, big waves rush at them. Pages of men follow, men in planes or with camels or in uniform. No Amelia Earhart. No Mary Reiby. No Truganini. In high school, no Miles Franklin, no Christina Stead. This was in the 1950s and 1960s, when many of the poets in this book were at school.

Finding poems from our colonial ancestors of the nineteenth century was almost as difficult as finding song texts in translation. We have read Mary Gilmore. Who were the other women poets writing before Judith Wright began publishing?

Some names — Zora Cross   Ada Cambridge   Lesbia Harford Anna Wickham   Ricketty Kate   Ethel Anderson   Mary Fullerton ('E') Anonymous   Dorothea Mackellar   Eve Langley   Marie Pitt.

They often wrote with great sexual and social honesty. Their voices are clear and witty. They were experimenting with the forms and themes of poetry, and they were politically concerned. Ada Cambridge, a novelist as well as a poet, has been described by H. M. Green as 'the first Australian writer, of prose or verse, to whom social problems really mattered.'[20] The writing of Mary Gilmore, Mary Fullerton, Anna Wickham, Lesbia Harford and Marie Pitt overlaps with the early labour and suffrage movements with the work of people like Vida Goldstein, Rose Scott, Alice Henry and Miles Franklin. The tradition of left feminist writing in Australia is submerged in most histories and curricula, yet the ideas have been important in shaping women's consciousness of language and the subjects we choose to write about.

The early poets talk about the selector's wife and daughter, about miners, slum children, prostitutes, machinists in factories, period pain, cars, cigarettes, sex, social conventions, strikes, feminism, lovers, Japan, female convicts, kissing, old age, gadgets, India, happy marriage, rhyme, women lovers, the Harbour Bridge.

Ada Cambridge (1844-1926), married to the Reverend G. E. Cross, was able to say:

> I kiss; I feast; but I am hungry still

and

> . . . I would not dare pretend
> To constant passion and a lifelong trust

but her book *Unspoken Thoughts*, published in London in 1887, was suppressed, since it was thought to be so outspoken that it would hinder her husband's career.[21]

Mary Gilmore (1865-1962) published more widely than Ada Cambridge. Her poems which relate most directly to women's lives are not usually included in anthologies; she is better remembered for *Old Botany Bay*.

Anna Wickham (1884-1947) grew up in Australia. At the age of twenty she went to England to further her career, both as a poet and as an operatic singer. She gave up singing to marry a scientist, and for five years played the difficult role of a model wife to a conventional husband. When the feeling of suffocation became too strong, she began to write poetry in secret. When the poems were published, 'Anna, feeling excited and triumphant, showed them to her husband. He was very angry, thought anything she wrote worthless, and in any case had no intention of allowing his wife to be a poet. She was not to do it again. Anna exploded with rage and found herself certified as insane.'[22]

Zora Cross (1890-1964) wrote with a kind of hothouse sexuality about her lovers and her husband, and had a reputation as an accomplished sonnet writer. The first edition of *Songs of Love and Life*, published when she was 'quite young', sold out in three days. The copy held at the Mitchell Library contains handwritten comments by Christopher Brennan, who knew more about usage, commas and craft. 'Poetry doesn't need exclamation marks.' He suggested Cross substitute 'wherein' for 'where', 'thence' for 'there', 'thronged' for 'heaped' and 'clasped' for 'held'. Beside the poem 'Thou Shalt Not' (page 24) he wrote 'What does it all mean, anyhow?' and 'Doors creak: but does anything ever creak through a door?'

Men come from a different place, their journeys are different from ours. I wouldn't allow myself to be seriously influenced by a male critic of my work. This is because I believe that men are frequently uncomfortable with women's writing and this discomfort is not owned as such, but dissembled into criticism. I don't mean this is always the case. But we need to be aware of the possiblity when we listen to male comments on our writing, and trust again and again, only our own inner voice.

All my life I have directed my energy outwards. This is how we have been taught to live, to anticipate the demands of others. Now for the first time I am learning to direct this energy inwards. The other day I was making strawberry milkshakes for five children in my kitchen. I was hardly aware of them. I was thinking about a story I'm writing. It was wonderful to realise later the achievement of detachment I was moving towards.

Jennifer Wilson, 1986

A contemporary male critic and poetry editor who has been influenced by feminist theory gives this account of the way he used to read women's poetry.

I have begun to think that I might have been quite wrong in many of my suggestions, quite blind in my rejection of poems that, because they did not conform in sufficient respects to what I had come to believe were the fundamentals of good poetry, I thought were poor or inept or somehow simply misconceived . . . if *I* was doing that, and in some small way helping to repress a way of saying that I did not understand or for which I could not see the necessity, how many others must have been doing likewise, and for how long?'[23]

David Brooks, 1985

a picture of history

There is a photograph. The bearded faces are in three rows, they look sternly at the camera as people did in the days before smiling was a photographic fashion. Behind and between the solid bodies of the men are moving shadows. As the shapes come into focus the picture dissolves, the picture must be taken again.

Who was Ethel Anderson? Born in England in 1883, she was fifth-generation Australian. She was educated at Picton and later in Sydney. She moved in vice-regal and military circles, and for a time lived in India with her administrator husband. Slightly deaf in her later years, she flourished an immense silver ear trumpet draped with tulle. Nancy Keesing remembers her as a grand, eccentric woman whose personal style was after the fashion of her writing style – if her hat had wheat and French flowers, her ear trumpet had too.

Ethel Anderson was a poet and short story writer. John Douglas Pringle, who edited *The Best of Ethel Anderson: Tales of Parramatta and India* (1973) says 'I do not know of a better short story in Australian literature than 'Mrs James Greene'.[24] He describes Anderson as

a considerable scholar, knowing a little Greek and a lot of Latin. She was well read in French as well as English literature and especially admired Verlaine, Lamartine, Violette Leduc and . . '. Colette. She was also . . . an accomplished pianist, a keen amateur painter and a discerning critic of contemporary art.

Why is she so little known, either as poet or short story writer? Pringle's view is that:

Australians could not believe that anyone who had spent much of her social life in and around Government House could be a serious writer (she was), let alone that, when her husband died in 1949, she might have to write for a living (she did).

Who was Lesbia Harford? She was writing during World War I and until her early death in 1927. A new edition of her work appeared in 1985, edited by Drusilla Modjeska and Marjorie Pizer. Before that, there had only been the limited edition edited by Nettie Palmer in 1941. Drusilla Modjeska writes:

Lesbia Harford graduated in law from Melbourne University, but she never practised. Instead she worked in textile and clothing factories and joined the I.W.W., the radical labour movement.

She is known more or less dimly to some poets and critics, beyond that barely at all, although one of her poems, 'Periodicity', is sung by the Adelaide band *Redgum* on their album *Virgin Ground:* 'Women, I say,/Are beautiful in change,/ Remote, immortal, like the moon they range.' (1917)

Her poems, many of them written as songs, raise critical questions of the relationship between popular and literary traditions of writing, the forms of protest poetry and the interconnections between histories of writing, class and feminism. These issues and the necessary re-readings that accompany them have become central to contemporary critical debates. [25]

Another area of re-reading concerns the lesbian voice. When a woman writes about sexual love for another woman, critics often assume that the voice is a male persona. In many cases including contemporary ones, the poet is speaking literally,[26] as Harford does.

Harford's first love affair, at least what seems to have been her first, serious love affair, was with a woman, an intense and absorbing relationship which lasted in some form until her death. Lesbia's lover, Katie Lush, was a philosophy tutor at Melbourne University. Katie and Lesbia made a striking pair, the one tall and red-headed, the other small and dark. Together they were members of the Victorian Socialist Party . . . [and were active in] the anti-conscription campaigns. In Lesbia's poems to Katie Lush, and . . . to [another friend and lover] Guido Baracchi, she reworks that contradictory set of emotions between love and independence.

Of the historical poets, Lesbia Harford and Anna Wickham are probably the closest in mood and subject matter to contemporary poets who form the bulk of the anthology. In 1916 it was extraordinary for women to be writing about their bodies, politics or class. It was unusual for poets to write beyond the constraints of nationalism.

Reputations have always been created for women poets which pigeonhole them into acceptable places. Mary Gilmore we have mentioned, Dorothea Mackellar is known only for 'My Country'. She also wrote the imagist 'Japanese Songs' and poems about the gender war: 'Arms and the Woman' deals with the same themes as Sylvia Kantaris' 'News from the Front' and Dipti Saravanamuttu's 'Statistic for the New World'.

The new world of Judith Wright's poetry — the politically concerned later poems — is also suppressed by anthologists in favour of her earlier, over-anthologised poems such as 'Woman to Man'. Wright requested that we choose from her later work, because it seems no one can hear her present voice. We may know and love 'South of My Days' and 'Bullocky', but few readers are familiar with 'At a Poetry Conference, Expo '67', or 'Report of a Working Party'.

what's happening now

Today there are critics who understand that aesthetic judgement is political, that your sexual politics and your class position have an effect on what poems you like. There are growing numbers of academics, men as well as women, who are 'working to expose the system of power that authorises certain representations while blocking, prohibiting or invalidating others.'[27]

We hope this book challenges the usual meaning of the term 'Australian poet' and opens possibilities for the range of contemporary writing.

It may be that our historical moment is the moment of speaking to the creators of popular imagery surrounding women, in voices that say

> It is the grief of angels to have to belch
> into each other's faces for excitement
> > Judy Beveridge, 1982

> After all
> I'd rather be a lover than a saint
> > Lesbia Harford, 1919

> I'm no sweet virgin sock-washer either
> > Vicki Viidikas, 1972

What else can be heard in these poems? Speaking about women's art practices, Anne-Marie Sauzea-Boetti has said:

The actual creative project of woman as subject involves betraying the oppressive
mechanisms of culture in order to express herself through the break, within the
gaps between the systematic spaces of artistic language . . . Not the project of fixing
meanings but of breaking them up and multiplying them.[28]

Susan Hampton and Kate Llewellyn

ABORIGINAL SONGS

from WUDAL-MAIMAI SONG SEQUENCE

Bambudmi yuru-yuru eee Ngurmili ngalia-giyin wangaa
wanga-ngu Bambudmi-ngu Bambula-ngu Lalamandja-ngu ee Ngurmi-
    ngurmi Gundjimul-ngu
eee yelala giyin wangaa Bambudmi-ngu
nyagnyag-bunum giyin-waa . . .
Djerambal wangaa daraag Ngudngud Gurgayubdun-ngu . . .
waguu laidjinii waguu miil waguu daraa-gunyau-rinya-rau
marga-miri ligan-djirlbangi waguu rumbaal wunye'yun
eee wangaa Ngurmilii Lalamandjaa Djerambal-ngaa . . .
gungdu bunarei djanbul-djanbul magariin-bunarei
yulguu duwaliin djirgaruwaa ngurumal-gaa . . .?
wararaa gwigdunawii wararaa . . . djurwarag mandulba-mandulbaa
nyagnyag-bunum Djeramba-lili Gurgayubdun-lili –
wagu-waguu wagu-waa waguu marga-miri . . . mulg-lilii
yaga ngaragu wagu kaana ngoi ngaragun gumurbwi . . .

Ah, the Wongar bird is speaking, through Djambarbingu country,
There at Bambudmi, at Bambula and Lalamandja, Ngurmi-ngurmi,
    Gundjimul.
Soon he will call out, through all those places . . .
Hear the cry of the bird!
There at Djerambal, and Ngudngud and Gurgayubdun . . .
Ah, my daughter's face! Her eyes! My daughter, there alone!
My daughter, her limbs and body dead and lost to me!
Ah, there at Ngurmili, Lalamandja and Djerambal . . .
The blood-red sky at sunset!
Whose is that mark, that sign on his face?
The djurwarag bird, he spits at the setting sun and the red sky.
His voice goes out to Djerambal and Gurgayubdun –
Ah my daughter, my daughter! . . . and to the sacred shade . . .
You are lying all alone, no longer close to my breast!

Comments:

'The song from which the extract is taken comes from the Wudal-Maimaia sequence, that is closely related to the *dua* Wawalag myth and song cycle. The brown djurwarag bird calls out at sunset when it sees the red sky that symbolizes menstrual blood, and the blood of the Wawalag sisters, or the blood of kangaroos killed and eaten by men in Wawalag country, far inland. The version here is Djambarbingu.

The singer, D. -, was a yiridja Dayur'yur woman whose mother was Djambarbingu, like D. - 's husband, B. -, the dead child's father. She was weeping for this child, her only daughter, who was just starting to crawl.'

from North-Eastern Arnhem Land

Naadiri numa lugayana-mii? Nganabru wagurinyin . . . Wani ngara lagarangu ngati-miringu waid-gurgu ngadili. Ngara yindi maragaridj, ngara yindi maragaridj! Naa ngaragu yudu, barba? Wunggaan? Ngaii gung-miri duwali! Dju'yuru ngara gawal-wirinyin wo'waid-naa . . . gabu lugiyei (namaa) . . . Yaguya ngaraya niniraa, baaraag! Waguu ngara gulgurau. Ding'waid! Gurugu djamarguli-na waangi! Daramu-na ngara wangiya! Ding'waid! Gurugu ngareya wandirii, wirigi ngareya waniya Marmin-ngura Liwa-liwadab-lari wanga, gawal-miringu-waid! . . . Yaga nii bragbragdun bapa-miringu. Wiribu ngara ngaama yulngu-maa. Gurugu niya bragbragdun-duru baari-yulgaraa miyalg-gara, yaga nguni niniya . . . Liandja ding-nguu malgmalg lia djalgdjalg-dunawi! Ngaragu duwali waguna luga djug, mambu-guduu . . . Ngara yaga ngura galgi G. -. Nii yaga djaal ngaragu, mainmag, ngara yaga nungu djaal! Ngara mardji galgi bapa, galgi ngaragu waanga. Naa nii, bunggawa? Naa nii, balanda? . . . Numa-na nugan-miri, aa yudu walgan-miri nganabrunggu dulmi'ya-djiri naaguna numa? Ngareya yaga bidjan! Danggi'yun aa bidji'yun guru-gama lambariyu, bai! Kaana waandirii! aa nganabrunggu wagu-rinyurau luga-na djug! Nii djaal, G. -. miyalg-goi darwa, mainmag, nii manngu darwa nungu wirgul-na, nii gaama nguni miyalg duwala waanga-lili, gurubulu darwa ngada . . . dju'yuru ngara galga-na . . . yuwalg ngara wangandja, daaya ngara wanga muga, gara ngara nyal'yun - yaga, yuwalg ninii! Yagana nyal'yun-dja! . . .

How can all you people go on eating and smoking, when our child - oh, I'll go, straightaway, and tell my father! I am angry, really angry! What is my daughter, is she rotten and stinking? Is she a wild dog? No, she's a human being! I'll send my uncle and my brothers here (to attack you all)! I'll put poison into your drinking water! I shan't stay here, I'm off to the west! No, I'll wait for my daughter's bones. [1] You women! All your children are alive! Men, I'm speaking to you! You women! I'll leave here as soon as I can, indeed I will! I'll go to my country, to Marmin-ngura, and Liwa-liwadab-lari. I'll get my uncles! As for you, G. -, you didn't sing for your child, as a father should do! I heard other people singing, but not you! All the singing you did was to lie down with some woman, not sitting down over there (where the others were singing)! . . . You are silly in the head from playing about with women, you're a fool! Oh, the maggots are eating my child![2] . . . I'm not going to sleep with G. –. You don't want me, G. –, good, I don't want you! I'm going away to my father, to my own country. What are you, G. – (to behave like that), a 'boss'? A white man? . . . All you others, you copulate and make children, why were you jealous of our child? I'm not like that (jealous of your children). You carry a child in paper-bark under your arm, then carry it at the back of your neck, on your shoulders – yes, and then it starts to run about by itself – ah, the maggots are eating our child! G. –, you want plenty of young girls! All right, you get all your young girls and bring them all here, and feed them up . . . (But) I'm going to send 'poison' here (for you all). I'm telling the truth, I'm not just pretending! No, indeed, what I'm telling you is true! . . .

Comments:
'The speaker was Y. –, a Ridarngu-speaking woman married to her third husband, a Marangu-speaking man, G. –. (These are dialects in the north-eastern Arnhem Land constellation, where marriage rules stipulate that people had to marry outside their own set of named dialect and clan groups. Y. – had been deeply upset by the death of her youngest child, a small girl named Mararawi. She did not utter the girl's name, because of the name-tabu following a death. But usually a woman would not use her husband's name (or a man use his wife's name) publicly, as she did here, except in times of stress and anger. She vented her anger on her husband, accusing him of showing too much interest in other women. In particular, she was jealous of his latest wife, a young girl who had not yet reached puberty . . . Y. – carried on much of her monologue in a mixed-Djambarbingu dialect of the *dua* moiety (set of dialect-clan groups); her husband was *dua*, like her own mother, a Djinba-Mandalbwi woman from the west, towards Milingimbi; and so were her uncles, her mother's brothers. (Y. – and her brothers were *yiridja* like their father and father's fathers.)'

[1.] She will certainly leave the place, she says, but first she must wait until her child's bones have been exhumed. The child had been given a Christian burial at the Mission Station, but it was planned to dig up the bones without the missionary's knowledge after about three weeks had elapsed.

[2.] The traditional practice in north-eastern Arnhem Land was to put the body of a dead person on a mortuary platform, while the appropriate clan songs were sung to help the soul or spirit on its way to the land of the dead. Later the bones would be collected and ritually sung over as they were put into specially prepared hollow-log 'coffins' painted with the dead person's clan designs. Women used the clan songs as a basis for their own commentaries and improvisations on these and other occasions.

ANONYMOUS

The Female Transport

[handwritten: Displays the strengths and limitations of the moralistic broadsheet ballad.]

Come all young girls, both far and near, and listen unto me,
While unto you I do unfold what proved my destiny,
My mother died when I was young, it caused me to deplore,
And I did get my way too soon upon my native shore.

Sarah Collins is my name, most dreadful is my fate,
My father reared me tenderly, the truth I do relate,
Till enticed by bad company along with many more,
It led to my discovery upon my native shore.

My trial it approached fast, before the judge I stood,
And when the judge's sentence passed it fairly chilled my blood,
Crying, 'You must be transported for fourteen years or more,
And go from hence across the seas unto Van Diemen's shore.'

It hurt my heart when on a coach I my native town passed by;
To see so many I did know, it made me heave a sigh;
Then to a ship was sent with speed along with many more,
Whose aching hearts did grieve to go unto Van Diemen's shore.

The sea was rough, ran mountains high, with us poor girls 'twas hard,
No one but God to us came nigh, no one did us regard.
At length, alas! we reached the land, it grieved us ten times more,
That wretched place Van Diemen's Land, far from our native shore.

They chained us two by two, and whipped and lashed along,
They cut off our provisions if we did the least thing wrong;
They march us in the burning sun until our feet are sore,
So hard's our lot now we are got to Van Diemen's shore.

We labour hard from morn to night until our bones do ache,
Then every one they must obey, their mouldy beds must make;
We often wish when we lay down we ne'er may rise no more
To meet our savage Governor upon Van Diemen's shore.

Every night when I lay down I wet my straw with tears,
While wind upon that horrid shore did whistle in our ears,

Those dreadful beasts upon that land around our cots do roar,
Most dismal is our doom upon Van Diemen's shore.

Come all young men and maidens, do bad company forsake,
If tongue can tell our overthrow it will make your heart to ache;
Young girls I pray be ruled by me, your wicked ways give o'er,
For fear like us you spend your days upon Van Diemen's shore.

ADA CAMBRIDGE

Desire.

Bright eyes, sweet lips, with many fevers fill
   The young blood, running wildly, as it must;
   But lips and eyes beget a strange distrust.
Electric fingers send the sudden thrill
Through senses unsubservient to the will;
   The flames die down, and leave a dim disgust;
   Unfragrant kisses turn to drouth and dust;
I kiss; I feast; but I am hungry still.

O woman, woman, passionate but strong!
   True to thy love as needle to the pole –
     True to the truth, and not alone to me –
O mate and friend, elusive in the throng,
     With thy clear brows, they straight and upright soul,
      Nameless – unknown – my hunger is for thee!

Vows.

Nay, ask me not. I would not dare pretend
   To constant passion and a life-long trust.
   They will desert thee, if indeed they must.
How can we guess what Destiny will send –
Smiles of fair fortune, or black storms to rend
   What even now is shaken by a gust?
   The fire will burn, or it will die in dust.
We cannot tell until the final end.

And never vow was forged that could confine
   Aught but the body of the thing whereon
Its pledge was stamped. The inner soul divine,
   That thinks of going, is already gone.
When faith and love need bolts upon the door,
Faith is not faith, and love abides no more.

What?

My children cry to me for bread,
And I, what can I do?
I *cannot bear that* they should starve,
You who reproach me, could you?

I cannot bear that they should sink
And die before my eyes,
Or cling to me with shrunken hands,
And stab me with their cries –

'Mam-ma'! . . . 'Mamma'! . . . day and night –
And, just outside, the street.
How can I help it? . . . Let me go:
They must have bread to eat.

The Woman

I am not very patient,
Yet patient I must be
With him beside my pillow
And the babe upon my knee.

I am not very patient,
I would have wings to fly,
Yet I am tied to cradles
Until the day I die.

One is a rocking cradle.
(Sleep babe, without alarms.)
And for the other baby,
The cradle of my arms.

Strange that I was given
Thoughts that soar to heaven,
Yet I must sit and keep
Children in their sleep.

Awakened

His eyes looked into mine,
   (O, look that made me wise!)
I hid my own, although
   My world lay in his eyes.

I turned away my face,
   My breath came like a sob;
And to his heart my own
   Gave answer, throb for throb.

I could not raise my eyes,
   Lest he should read therein;
And trembled, woman-wise,
   And woman-waked, within.

The Kiss

Lean over the fence and kiss? Not I!
   If the tide leapt up to a kiss
   The fence were a bar too low,
Or the kiss was a lie!
   And a kiss that's a lie is none
   When everything's said and done.

Lean over the fence and kiss?
   Philander and play the fool?
Blood that is blood is hotter than this,
   Or life were easy to school!

Lean over the fence and kiss? I? Never!
   Scorn to your Safe-to-lean-over,
   Half-and-half lover!
Give me the kiss that is all –
Or nothing forever.

Marri'd

It's singin' in an' out,
  An' feelin' full of grace;
Here 'n' there, up an' down,
  An' round about th' place.

It's rollin' up your sleeves,
  An' whit'nin' up the hearth,
An' scrubbin' out th' floors,
  An' sweepin' down th' path;

It's bakin' tarts an' pies,
  An' shinin' up th' knives;
An' feelin' 's if some days
  Was worth a thousand lives.

It's watchin' out th' door,
  An' watchin' by th' gate;
An' watchin' down th' road,
  An' wonderin' why he's late;

An' feelin' anxious-like,
  For fear there's something wrong;
An' wonderin' why he's kep',
  An' why he takes so long.

It's comin' back inside
  An' sittin' down a spell,
To sort o' make believe
  You're thinkin' things is well.

It's gettin' up again
  An' wand'rin' in an' out;
An' feelin' wistful-like,
  Not knowin' what about;

An' flushin' all at once,
  An' smilin' just so sweet,
An' feelin' real proud
  The place is fresh an' neat.

An' feelin' awful glad
    Like them that watch'd Silo'm;
An' everything because
    A man is comin' Home!

Honing up the Hill

Blue were the waters,
And bluer was the sky,
Warm was the clover,
Where the lambs loved to lie;
Not a sound I heard.
In the morning so still,
But an old woman honing,
Honing up the hill.

'Ochone!' she cried,
'Ochone-a-rie!
Bitter were the years
That got the best of me;
Once I had beauty,
And love that came at will,
Now I'm but an old woman,
Honing up the hill.'

'Glory be,' says I
To the old woman there,
'Can't you see the lark
With his wings on the air?'
Says she to me, then,
'You've got youth to your fill,
But I'm an old bent woman,
Honing up the hill.

'Honing up the hill,
And my back to the sun,
Honing up the hill
Where the long shadows run;

Once I had beauty,
And lovers asked my will,
Now I'm but an old grey woman,
Honing up the hill.'

Old Botany Bay

I'm old
Botany Bay;
Stiff in the joints,
Little to say.

I am he
Who paved the way,
That you might walk
At your ease today;

I was the conscript
Sent to hell
To make in the desert
The living well;

I bore the heat,
I blazed the track –
Furrowed and bloody
Upon my back.

I split the rock;
I felled the tree:
The nation *was* –
Because of me!

Old Botany Bay
Taking the sun
From day to day . . .
Shame on the mouth
That would deny
The knotted hands
That set us high!

MARY FULLERTON ('E')

Gadgets

This is a world of gadgets,
Neat, and fiendishly cunning;
One will do ten men's work,
And keep indefinitely running
On a meagre ration of oil.

How long will God bother with men,
When there are gadgets enough,
To do all the jobs of the world –
Formed out of the same raw stuff?

I see an eventual heaven,
Where the steel saints are screaming their praise
And composite angels wing-folded –
All breaks-down forgiven –
Are shriven, and soldered.

Immortal from dust,
Ransomed from rust,
Synthetic seraphs
Making joyous discord in heaven,
Allelujah, Allelujah!
Aluminium, Aluminium!
For ever, and ever, and ever.

Puppets

Why bring *him* here?
To this foul lane,
Where husbands know beer,
And wives know pain.

They've nothing to learn
From a puppet's knack:
Who drink half they earn,
Know how to thwack.

Old as old oak,
Punch beating his mate,
And – heart-breaking joke –
Quite up-to-date.

Threads

I watched a spider spin
A mystic rope
Made from his very self
And hope.

I saw a human soul
By a gulf stand,
Praying the farther side
Be land.

The spider's filament
Reached stem from sod;
The thread the soul flung forth
Reached God.

Lion

There was no ceremony
When the last god died,
No dramatic moment
When a new Faith slew;
But slow, undeified,
The once feared and cherished,
Outworn, forgotten,
Lion Life never knew
When the last god perished.

What next shall he lose
In his large going?
Leaves flung from his flanks
In terrible unknowing!

Humility

The poet was exuberant,
Along his labyrinth shouting.
'Good fellow, you must trim,'
The critics came a-clouting.

And so he cut and pruned,
At the behesting . . .
And now remain no bowers,
Nor sweet birds nesting.

ETHEL ANDERSON

Three Satires

I

I sit by the Tranquil River;
Looking in the eight directions – snow;
On the eastern edges – ice-hummocks.

Woebegone, I sent to the sunrise
A memorandum imploring aid;
I have reason to suppose it unread.

To the bird that sits cracking stars
On the Saëna tree – my appeal?
Unanswered. What has been my mistake?

Alas, alas! My name is unknown
In the Cloud Terraces. In vain
I bring myself to the notice of the Fortunate Ones.

II

Between one hunger and the next – three hours.
Between one book and the last – three years.
How can I expect my pen to satisfy my stomach?
I will go to Bombay and become a gaslight lady.

Sweet as a trail of honeysuckle
Frail and slender the gaslight ladies
Sway past on tentative feet,
Pearls in their ears, long gold hair,
Silver fox-pelts soothing an unfelt shame,
With my white locks, groping on two sticks,
In this competition – what hope have I?
I think – 'I'll go back to Gingerlee
And buy a new bottle of – bottle of?
And buy a new bottle of – ink.'

III

Thrusts, from Calcutta to Kabul, the Grand Trunk Road;
Blows, from west to east, fiercely, the autumn tornado;
Who is this battling woman with the twig besom
From sunrise to sunset sweeping against the wind?

The Grand Trunk Road trails right across Asia;
The Banyan leaves litter the bitter sky;
The Indian dust presages – soon, soon, the Earth-moon;
Who is this creature of so much hope, so little wisdom?
It is Sucreete, the ryot's wife, earning five annas.

ANNA WICKHAM

The Sick Assailant

I hit her in the face because she loved me.
It was the challenge of her faithfulness that moved me.
For she knew me, every impulse, every mood,
As if my veins had run with her heart's blood.
She knew my damned incontinence, my weakness,
Yet she forebore with her accursed meekness.
I could have loved her had she ever blamed me,
It was her sticky irritating patience shamed me.
I was tired-sick. It was her business to amuse me,
Her faith could only daunt me and confuse me.
She was a fine great wench, and well I knew
She was one good half panther, one half shrew,
Then why should my love, more than any other,
Induce in her the silly human Mother?
She would have nursed me, bathed me, fed me, carried me.
She'd have burned her soul to thaw me, she'd have married me.
I hit her in the face because she loved me,
It was her sticky irritating patience moved me.

Note on Rhyme

Likeness of sound,
With just enough of difference
To make a change of sense;
So we have contrast,
A piquancy,
And a certain victory of contrivance.
But Heaven keep us from an inevitable rhyme,
Or from a rhyme prepared!

Rhymed verse is a wide net
Through which many subtleties escape.
Nor would I take it to capture a strong thing,
Such as a whale.

The Fired Pot

In our town, people live in rows.
The only irregular thing in a street is the steeple;
And where that points to God only knows,
And not the poor disciplined people!

And I have watched the women growing old,
Passionate about pins, and pence, and soap,
Till the heart within my wedded breast grew cold,
And I lost hope.

But a young soldier came to our town,
He spoke his mind most candidly.
He asked me quickly to lie down,
And that was very good for me.

For though I gave him no embrace –
Remembering my duty –
He altered the expression of my face,
And gave me back my beauty.

The Marriage

What a great battle you and I have fought!
A fight of sticks and whips and swords,
A one-armed combat,
For each held the left hand pressed close to the
      heart,
To save the caskets from assault.

How tenderly we guarded them;
I would keep mine and still have yours,
And you held fast to yours and coveted mine.
Could we have dropt the caskets
We would have thrown down weapons
And been at each other like apes,
Scratching, biting, hugging
In exasperation.

What a fight!
Thank God that I was strong as you,
And you, though not my master, were my match.
How we panted; we grew dizzy with rage.
We forgot everything but the fight and the love of
      the caskets.

These we called by great names –
Personality, Liberty, Individuality.

Each fought for right to keep himself a slave
And to redeem his fellow.
How can this be done?

But the fight ended.
For both was victory
For both there was defeat.
Through blood we saw the caskets on the floor.
Our jewels were revealed;
An ugly toad in mine,
While yours was filled with most contemptible
      small snakes:
One held my vanity, the other held your sloth.

The fight is over, and our eyes are clear. –
Good friend, shake hands.

DOROTHEA MACKELLAR

Two Japanese Songs

1.

THE HEART OF A BIRD

What does the bird-seller know of the heart of a bird?

There was a bird in a cage of gold, a small red bird in a cage of gold.
The sun shone through the bars of the cage, out of the wide heaven.
The depths of the sky were soft and blue, greatly to be longed-for.
The bird sang for desire of the sky, and her feathers shone redder for
    sorrow:
And many passed in the street below, and they said one to another:
'Ah, that we had hearts as light as a bird's!'

But what does the passer-by know of the heart of a bird?

What does the bird-seller know of the heart of a bird?

'I have given grain for you to eat, and water that you may bathe.'
Shall not this bird be content? is there need to clip her wings?
No, for the cage is very strong, the golden bars are set close.
Yet the real bird has flown away, very far away over the rice-fields.
There is only the shadow-body in the cage.

What does the bird-seller care for the heart of a bird?

2.

A SMOKE SONG

There is a grey plume of smoke in the horizon,
The smoke of a steamer that has departed over the edge of the world.
There is the smoke of a dying fire in my heart,
The smoke has hurt my eyes, they ache with tears.

Arms and the Woman

What if I do go armed? she said.
   Where's the law that you say I've broken?
Firearms, yes – but my weapon's steel,
   A two-edged dagger, and more by token
Its supple keenness that seldom slips
Is mostly quiet behind my lips.

Life's not often a peaceful job,
   Enemies lurk or else attack you,
Horns well down in a daunting way –
   There's not always a friend to back you.
I am peaceable *sans* pretence:
That's not always enough defence.

Though the ewe be a gentle beast,
   Supercilious and yet a-tremble,
Deprecating and obstinate,
   She's not one that I would resemble.
Rather I'd be a tiger-cat,
Even an outlaw thing like that.

Friends or honour or self-respect –
   There are times when a weapon ready
(Often readiness is enough)
   Can defend them or keep them steady;
One may walk in a zone of charmed
Peace and courtesy, being armed.

Who can say that I struck him first?
   Many might think I love the quarrel,
Though it sickens me – yet at worst
   This pet folly may point a moral,
Women should lead a guarded life –
God be thanked, I carry a knife.

My Country

The love of field and coppice,
  Of green and shaded lanes,
Of ordered woods and gardens
  Is running in your veins.
Strong love of grey-blue distance
  Brown streams and soft, dim skies –
I know but cannot share it,
  My love is otherwise.

I love a sunburnt country,
  A land of sweeping plains,
Of ragged mountain ranges,
  Of droughts and flooding rains.
I love her far horizons,
  I love her jewel-sea,
Her beauty and her terror –
  The wide brown land for me!

The stark white ring-barked forests,
  All tragic to the moon,
The sapphire-misted mountains,
  The hot gold hush of noon.
Green tangle of the brushes,
  Where lithe lianas coil,
And orchids deck the tree tops
  And ferns the warm dark soil.

Core of my heart, my country!
  Her pitiless blue sky,
When sick at heart, around us,
  We see the cattle die –
But then the grey clouds gather,
  And we can bless again
The drumming of an army,
  The steady, soaking rain.

Core of my heart, my country!
  Land of the Rainbow Gold,
For flood and fire and famine,
  She pays us back three-fold.

Over the thirsty paddocks,
　　Watch, after many days,
The filmy veil of greenness
　　That thickens as we gaze . . .

An opal-hearted country,
　　A wilful, lavish land –
All you who have not loved her,
　　You will not understand –
Though earth holds many splendours,
　　Wherever I may die,
I know to what brown country
　　My homing thoughts will fly.

ZORA CROSS

Thou Shalt Not

Woman, pausing on the marble stair,
   Come down one . . . come down two;
Death is creaking through the doors of air,
   And a red, red knife for you.

Woman, lying on the gleaming floor,
   Warm the blade . . . cold your skin;
Love's a madman when he loves no more,
   And a heart is hot with sin.

from Love Sonnets

X.

And then came Science with her torch red-lit
And cosmic marvels round her glowing head –
The primal cell, the worm, the quadruped –
Striving to make each to the other fit.
Tongue-trumpeting her own unchallenged wit,
She offered me the woof of Wisdom's thread,
And Truth and Purity that hourly tread
The paths where sages in their wonder sit.

And still I smiled and kissed you with a sob.
My lips on yours, I heard, high up above
Love's feet ring laughter on the starry sod
And felt the echo through our bosoms throb.
Belovèd, Science ends in our pure love
Which shares alone the secrets of our God.

LESBIA HARFORD

Fatherless

I've had no man
To guard and shelter me,
Guide and instruct me
From mine infancy.

No lord of earth
To show me day by day
What things a girl should do
And what she should say.

I have gone free
Of manly excellence
And hold their wisdom
More than half pretence.

For since no male
Has ruled me or has fed,
I think my own thoughts
In my woman's head.

Sometimes I think the happiest of love's moments
Is the blest moment of release from loving.

The world once more is all one's own to model
Upon one's own and not another's pattern.

And each poor heart imprisoned by the other's
Is suddenly set free for splendid action.

For no two lovers are a single person
And lovers' union means a soul's suppression.

Oh, happy then the moment of love's passing
When those strong souls we sought to slay recover.
24/7/18

You want a lily
And you plead with me
'Give me my lily back.'

I went to see
A friend last night and on her mantle shelf
I saw some lilies,
Image of myself,
And most unlike your dream of purity.

They had been small green lilies, never white
For man's delight
In their most blissful hours.
But now the flowers
Had shrivelled and instead
Shone spikes of seeds,
Burned spikes of seeds,
Burned red
As love and death and fierce futurity.

There's this much of the lily left in me.
9/3/18

The Invisible People

When I go into town at half past seven
Great crowds of people stream across the ways,
Hurrying, although it's only half past seven.
They are the invisible people of the days.

When you go in to town about eleven
The hurrying, morning crowds are hid from view.
Shut in the silent buildings at eleven
They toil to make life meaningless for you.

Skirt Machinist

I am making great big skirts
For great big women –
Amazons who've fed and slept
Themselves inhuman.

Such long skirts, not less than two
And forty inches.
Thirty round the waist for fear
The webbing pinches.

There must be tremendous tucks
On those round bellies.
Underneath the limbs will shake
Like wine-soft jellies.

I am making such big skirts
And all so heavy,
I can see their wearers at
A lord-mayor's levee.

I, who am so small and weak
I have hardly grown,
Wish the skirts I'm making less
Unlike my own.

I can't feel the sunshine
Or see the stars aright
For thinking of her beauty
And her kisses bright.

She would let me kiss her
Once and not again.
Deeming soul essential,
Sense doth she disdain.

If I should once kiss her,
I would never rest
Till I had lain hour long
Pillowed on her breast.

Lying so, I'd tell her
Many a secret thing
God has whispered to me
When my soul took wing.

Would that I were Sappho,
Greece my land, not this!
There the noblest women,
When they loved, would kiss.
4/4/15

Periodicity

My friend declares
Being woman and virgin she
Takes small account of periodicity.

And she is right.
Her days are calmly spent
For her sex-function is irrelevant.

But I whose life
Is monthly broke in twain
Must seek some sort of meaning in my pain.

Women, I say,
Are beautiful in change
Remote, immortal, like the moon they range.

Or call my pain
A skirmish in the whole
Tremendous conflict between body and soul.

Meaning must lie,
Some beauty surely dwell
In the fierce depths and uttermost pits of hell.

Yet still I seek,
Month after month in vain,
Meaning and beauty in recurrent pain.

Via the Bridge

If you come often to Sydney via the Bridge
And have studied the racing notes
And scanned the headlines,
You may glance at the Cables
Or the crimson pointed nails
of the woman opposite.
But, if you have not passed that way before,
You will look at the Pylons
And you will say to yourself:
'How regular these pinnacles are,
And
How alien!'
And, when they are behind,
'I am treading upon the smoke
Of a ship that perhaps
Sailed out from Brazil;'
Or you will whisper to yourself:
'This is the way the winds walk
Above the sea.
Where the gulls flicker like silver moths.'
Then you will want to put your hands
Out of the window
And let them flutter
With all the things
That move above the waters.
And, when you are in the centre –
That enormous centre
Moulded of concrete and steel,
And the sweat of hands
And the labour of minds –
And there is nothing beneath
But the wind and the smoke and the gulls –
Nothing to the East and nothing to the West
But the miraculous web of the skies

Spun from the four horizons,
'This is a great wonder,'
Your spirit will sing:
'I shall not pass
This way again, too soon,
That I may keep
This vast astonishment.'

OLIVE HOPEGOOD

My Sister . . .

(My sisters, let us go mad for God. – St. Theresa.)

My sister, let us drink methylated spirits
out of the beautiful pliant glasses
whispering still
of the colour of canals.
      That will be a little shout
      beneath the plated cover.

Let us tread grapes in the streets
'till the red wine runs to the gutter.
Let us wear furs against our naked skins
and give to the rain and wind
white linen.
Let us toss up our febrile thoughts
against the uncoloured air
and sway with laughter,
Pretending to embrace.
      Let us pretend to shout
      beneath the plated cover.

My sister, let us be epicene
and run in wooden shoes
across the splintering echoes
of erotic tiles.
My sister, let us do anything
to forget that pain
traces white patterns
on a shivering glass,
that Lorca is dead
while we are full of shame
and madness sobs in the cafes
and the twisted lanes.

MARY FINNIN

Breaking Drought

My bones are cursed by centuries
Of Scottish mist and wild Atlantic gale;
So now in this dry land they still remember
In pain those far off days when never a tree
Could flourish, though black rock
Came gold with lichen on the southern steeps.
Small wonder that I long for the odd flood year
When all is bloom and paper daisies snow
From beery Bourke to mutton-chop Balranald.

EVE LANGLEY

Native-born

In a white gully among fungus red
    Where serpent logs lay hissing at the air,
I found a kangaroo. Tall, dewy, dead,
    So like a woman, she lay silent there.
Her ivory hands, black-nailed, crossed on her breast,
    Her skin of sun and moon hues, fallen cold.
Her brown eyes lay like rivers come to rest
    And death had made her black mouth harsh and old.
Beside her in the ashes I sat deep
    And mourned for her, but had no native song
To flatter death, while down the ploughlands steep
    Dark young Camelli whistled loud and long,
'Love, liberty, and Italy are all.'
    Broad golden was his breast against the sun.
I saw his wattle whip rise high and fall
    Across the slim mare's flanks, and one by one
She drew the furrows after her as he
    Flapped like a gull behind her, climbing high,
Chanting his oaths and lashing soundingly,
    While from the mare came once a blowing sigh.
The dew upon the kangaroo's white side
    Had melted. Time was whirling high around,
Like the thin wommera, and from heaven wide
    He, the bull-roarer, made continuous sound.
Incarnate lay my country by my hand:
    Her long hot days, bushfires, and speaking rains,
Her mornings of opal and the copper band
    Of smoke around the sunlight on the plains.
Globed in fire-bodies the meat-ants ran
    To taste her flesh and linked us as we lay,
For ever Australian, listening to a man
    From careless Italy, swearing at our day.
When, golden-lipped, the eagle-hawks came down
    Hissing and whistling to eat of lovely her,

And the blowflies with their shields of purple brown
  Plied hatching to and fro across her fur,
I burnt her with the logs, and stood all day
  Among the ashes, pressing home the flame
Till woman, logs, and dreams were scorched away,
  And native with night, that land from whence they came.

ELIZABETH RIDDELL

Occasions of Birds

I.

I heard on the radio how birds in Assam
lifted like a cloud over the camellia forest
and flew to a village in the last light.
There it was warm and filled with other wings
transparent and flickering.
They dashed themselves against the smoking lamps and fell
into the street
on to the trodden stems of water hyacinth.

Women who had been picking tea
all day on the hillside
came down to the village
holding their baskets against their muslin skirts
and their skirts away from the bleeding feathers
in fear and surprise. There was hardly a sound
when the wings ceased to beat.

It was south of the Kahsi hills where the Brahmaputra flows
the birds flowed to their death in the soft night.

II.

In Dar es Salaam the morning lay on us like wet silk.
We bought fruit in thin slices and yellow bead rings,
waiting for the news of the tornado, the hurricane,
the cyclone, the typhoon
crouched in the opaque sky.

We ran before the hurricane
to Malagasy, to Réunion, to Mauritius
where it caught us, cast us on the beach
beside the tourist cabins and the sugar cane,
both with rats.

Port Louis was under water, we saw with dismay.
The corpses of duck dinners

floated in the gutter under blind windows
and past the closed doors of schools.

Reflected in this aberrant lake, old cool houses
suitable for provincial nobles and for slaves
brooded under wisteria. Their columns were erected
in memory of the Loire.

I recalled reading about the pink pigeons of Mauritius.
They had tiny heads and supplicating voices,
poor flakes of pink driven out when the forest was felled
to make way for the chateaux.
There is not one left to complain.

III.
Governor Hunter despatched
many a live bird to England
to bleach in the fog, attempt a trill
in Hove or Lockerbie
and marvel through the bars
at rain on the pale honeyed flowers
and at honeyeaters dancing on the rain.

As Governor Hunter and his men marched west
the sun struck gold from epaulettes
and sparkled on the cages ready for the feather,
the bright eye, the tender claw, the beak
of the lyrebird and the cockatoo
(the rosy one, the sulphur-crested screamer, the shining black)
and the paradise parrot of which Leach says
'it is an exquisite creature,
in general green below and blue above'
(like forest, like sky)
'with red shoulders'
(at sunsest out-sparkling the Governor's gold)
'and a red forehead. It nests in sandhills.'

One hundred and eighty years later
a man is out there in the dunes
searching for the paradise parrot.
Listen as he walks, crab-scuttle on the sand.

He has not much to offer this bird
which saw the gold and heard the sound of fife and drum.

IV.

We were in a foreign country
reading in a newspaper about another foreign country –
well, hardly foreign at all
since once we saw it from a deck,
a smudge of cloud on cloud, Mangere Island in the lonely Chathams
twelve thousand miles away in the long fall
of grey seas. Reading about the five black robins
last of their race,
news beccause they were about to die.
As with a few Indians along the Amazon,
robins and Indians, the only news,
small items because so far away and small
and about to die.

Rain sluiced the colonnades
where they sold the International Herald Tribune
(how to rent a palazzo, share a car to Munich, learn Chinese)
with baseball scores from home.
Rare robins, the item said,
rare black robins, three females and two males.
The usual ratio, we're used to it.

It's cold on Mangere. The waves swing in across the rocks
great shawls of kelp.
Three men were on Mangere
with tents and paperbacks and Tarot cards
a radio, tinned butter, binoculars
to watch the robins, and suddenly spied
after fifteen years the orange-breasted parakeet
risen again, a flame rekindled from the phoenix fire.
What next? The black stilt or the kakapo?
The parrot like an owl that walks, stately, instead of flying?
We doubt if they'll turn up.

The birds will be reprogrammed. Not much to do
with chirping, building nests or catching gnats
or even flying. It's cold on Mangere
for orange-breasted parakeets and such.

Personal Notices

Seeing their listed names I place features on them,
eyes, mouth and nose, the occasional ear
decorated with a gold ring or sunburn. I place suits on them,
black suits on men who sit on bentwood chairs to play guitars,
and suits for drinking in half-empty bars
entered through bead curtains and peeling painted doors
over thresholds separating mud and rain
in gutters of twilight streets.

I place them in motor cars and planes and trains
or behind desks, arms folded, staring.
When they question me I always answer yes.
I place them in beds, spread in their own sweat on temporary
                              sheets.

I place them at lecterns, and beyond their expounding mouths
the resistant faces clenched against the word,
a band of iron around the brain, the pulse repeating in denial
not so, not so.

Seeing their listed names I place other names on them.
I place pens in their hands for them to write
in unfamiliar languages
company reports and postcards home, and letters beginning
'Why should I weep over the ruins of Palmyra?'

Sometimes I place tears on their cheeks
because they died mystified and unconsolable
at the long delay of expected happiness.

Kauri

Reminding me of the giant trees falling
bleeding red and yellow into the swamp
the tourist film shows (was it like that?)
a man splitting kauri into shingles
to make a roof to cover a wife and child
and the old mother and the fishing gear
and the fireplace and the rack for pipes.
The Maori's face is mild.
He endures. Was it like that?
When I grew up without knowing
I made of the pohutukawa and the rata vine
something else, something English out of a book,
Arthur and Lancelot and Guinevere.

Reminding me now, this film, of the giant trees falling
bleeding on to the mud and bracken.
There are the black and white cows who will not look,
their haunches turned against the act of death,
and in the dairy the youth morosely reading
old magazines with pictures of windmills and cottages.
A Barnardo boy stranded in kauri country
who later hanged himself.

Growing up I watched the sunrise
burn a mountain quivering with birds
but I was thinking of something English, something out of a book.

VERA NEWSOM

Bricks

To-day I cannot write a poem. I am in a brick cell.
It is empty.

I have measured the bricks with the span of my hand –
one span and a bit. Nine inches.

Do not ask me what it would measure in millimetres. One
day if I stay in this cell long enough I will tell you.

As it is, I brick-measure space and I brick-measure
time.

My cell is sixteen brick-measures long and nine brick-
measures wide.

I pace up and down in my cell. It is five paces long.
Space is sixteen brick-measures and five paces long.
And time?

I don't want to think about time. Is one brick an hour,
or a day or a month? Dare I count all the bricks in my
cell? Do they measure the length of my sentence? But
I sit in the middle of brickwork, I gaze at the brickwork, I count every brick.

Sometimes I stare at the grouting. The bricks are
colourless, mottled in black, white and grey; the
grouting is totally black.

I trace the furrow of the grating with my finger. Soon
it is raw and beginning to bleed. But my brickmill is
a treadmill. I cannot stop.

Deeper and deeper, I trace the line of the grouting.
No longer a furrow, it is a declivity, a chasm. And I?
I am a black river at the bottom of a black chasm.

But the river is flowing. Smoothly. The sleek dark
river runs smoothly.

Now it is tensing its sinews, is leaping a cliff face,
is racing round boulders and out into daylight.

It tosses its mane. Its mane flashes gold, a tawny red
gold. I clutch at its mane.

I am riding a lion, over oceans of grasses, blonde,
silver and green. Clumps of tree brush by me, rocks
on the horizon zoom past. Trees, grasses blur.

Space, time are wind-measured, unmeasured. I do not
mind which. I am speeding through space, beyond time.

Am I a lion, or riding a lion? Is my poem a lion? Does
my poem ride me?

BARBARA GILES

Fireworks and Champagne

I pass among you disguised, you'll scarcely see me
in this slack envelope, unremarkable,

heavy with the dull purviews of age,
warmth, the next meal, the next step.

Ah, if you knew, I am in my second childhood,
each flower incandescent, the sky bluer and bluer.

Spring is a star-burst, the trees whizz up like rockets,
the children are jumping-jacks, girls are fountains.

Such colour and sound, I shall shatter with joy,
leach into rivers, blow on the wind.

You can sweep me up, walk through me.
I am winning, I am becoming invisible.

Learning all the Words in the World
Baby, aged two

Walking accomplished, so much energy
goes into words. Each object named
with glee, each name a part of object,
each object recollectable by name
for her admiring listeners.

She sits on the edge of conversation,
practising. 'Shattered,' she says and 'Tipsy,'
'Wild goose chase,' 'Naive.' The talkers
glance at her and stop their talk of rape,
rummaging in memory for paradigms
of infant apperception. One recalls
fear, of a gaggle of geese, the other, blame,
defiance, ashes in the mouth.

They cease to scold, sweetening their words, but soon
they're back to what's more natural to them,
rapping the world from pot to politics.
The child turns pages carefully, intoning,
'Apple: fish: jaguar: peacock: unicorn.'
Studious, prim, 'Nuclear war,' she says.

JOYCE LEE

Miriol

1

Winked at by stars, Miriol's smallness
Walks away to the open country of yellow moons.
From childhood's props outgrown, carrying
shoulder-packed desires,
the young girl leaves the white sleepout,
wistaria-covered veranda,
the privet hedge filtering wagon dust.
She travels alone. Itinerants
teach how to mask a face, to voice more heart.

2

Round the campfire in the frosted wilderness,
the group sings drovers' songs to dingoes,
nomad ghosts rustle in Miriol's night.
Cold at sunrise, she overtakes
the cough-racked prospector
heading for a final dig in the abandoned mine.
She offers donkey work, a partnership.

Ten days the tunnel squeezes them
to unyielding bone with relics of props,
rotten timber, a shovel. Chipping hard
they believe in a worthwhile seam, the last day
dynamite seals the shaft.
The old man settled underground, she walks
toward distant peaks, a barrier
blue to blue, rises abruptly from the flatlands.

3

Lightning over the abyss
defines the clouds,
forks the gap's dark gully.

Listless men wait for reveille,
a grave-digger unsleeping
drops clods. Apart
chain saws are stacked, machinery rusts.

Ears pitch to groans,
peg no consonants to vowels.

Scarps rise to bare rock.
Through penetrating damp of fog
Miriol walks pursued,
a stick shelter torn by blizzards
slants to mountain barriers.
She sleeps
through the nightmares.

4

The devil's scraps
scattered like vegetables
seduce her. He balances
on the punchbowl's
lava slopes, and lighthanded
reaches for her pack.

 'I'll shoulder it, come
 sip my light.'

 'Thank you, no.
 I keep my soul
 there.'

They feast. Banked fires
keep them warm. He blows up
Miriol's complaint
into fireworks, igniting clouds.
Foot by foot, the runaway
climbs a barren chimney.
Three days on,
fog blots the mountains.
Revelation crackles connections
scorched in her head.
Sky blue, a cobweb hammock

funnels her, burning
into the slip-stream.
No shrinking, no blackening.
No ash.

5

Homesick for the plains, she slides cold hands
through her grandfather's hot bagged wheat.
A bush fire envelops her, sweat-soaked
volunteers beat madly for nothing.
Morning. Dogs bark at cars
settling in shade beside the house.
    'We'll fix the fences, be finished by lunch.'
After the drought, they re-hang doors,
plaster cracks. With rain the ground recovers,
overflows in seven bumper years.

6

Mountains lift. Blue explodes orange-lit
over the trees, the sun, a golden wheel,
spokes the peaks. Night's forerunners
grow dark fingers. An elderly full face,
clear of clouds, drops unreturnable paths.
Baggageless now, she walks
in the open country of yellow moons.

Dreams for Wheat

Wheatland pioneers, they camp a night
beside the swamp, Gentleman Johann
trading a weedless slice of Germany
for flies and dust, black mud clay. Dreaming
Caroline transplants willows from Silesia.

She sleeps uneasily on the wagon-bed, uncertainties
shuffle over frosty grass, horses stamp.
A mopoke mourns for lost landowners
watching beyond the fire. Waterbirds call morning.
They divide land for farms around the swamp.

Crops carry the wind on brolga plains. Caroline
raises turkey flocks and children,
counts bagged gold in paddocks. They thatch
a schoolhouse, build a church. Its bell
rings prayers, tolls their crossing into heaven.

Their swamp drought-dry, farmers and horses
plough and scoop, heap an island for nests.
Fishermen build a jetty. The doctor's wife
boils coppers of cincona bark, then plants
silver poplar glades, Caroline's dream willows.

Reddened in Krakatoa's sunsets, with iron buckets
she waters avenues of gum trees, my inheritance.
Caroline comforts my uneasy sleep,
I'm watcher and watched, waiting on edges of the dark
for morning's first light across the plains.

MARY DURACK

Lament for the Drowned Country

You hear them kids over there laugh this old woman?
'She mad, old Maggie. She sit there fishing all day –
talk to myself and when she got a catch she let him go.
We *seen* her let'em go.
Mad Maggie! Mad Maggie! Poor old *Jilligan, Numbajina,*
Mad Maggie. You look now – she let that fish go . . .'

They can laugh at me, old Maggie, old *Jilligan* –
Numbajina skin woman belong *Mirriwung* tribe.
I don't expect young people understand –
not these days – understand. They got different singing –
all that pop-song – good too! I like'm too.
And all that cowboy picture – Red Indian fella . . .
Well that all right. That good too. When I been young girl
I ride like cowboy with them cattle, all same man –
only nothing Indian – nothing feather. Aboriginal different.
He only sing out 'Yakai! Yakai!' Like-a-that.
Djoalung – blackfellow people – more quiet people – my people.
I got to remember that *Djoalung*, that dreamtime people
I got to remember *Moolarli, Bilbilji, Yarralong,*
I got to remember *Beermun, Gudwirri* – big spirit song men.
I got to talk them old fellas – send 'em that message.

I sit along river coming down from my born country.
That heart place! I got to talk to that water.
I got to tell that fish: 'You go back – go back now –
talk strong my country. You tell him that spirit can't leave 'em.
You tell him – Wait! Hang on! *This not the finish!*
Bilbilji, grasshopper fella on top that mountain –
you tell him: Don't go away. You tell him my old man
still got him that corroboree where him lift him wing
Brrr! Brrr! Brrr! He keep that corroboree – can't lose'm'.
Moolarli – Oooo – strong fellow that one for making country.
All that good spring water for wallaby, cattle, everything –
Moolarli make'm. You know that old station waterhole?

In-bulling-burry we call'm. Whiteman call'm *Argyle.*
Well, that where 'im come from first time. Nothing whiteman
when *Moolarli* jump up from waterhole, move round in whirlwind
like helicopter. (*You-eye,** he got that helicopter first time –
before whiteman). He got spear like lightning – flash one – like fire.
All right, one day he come along – only billabong that time –
nothing river. He see old Jabiroo alonga water –
fishin', fishin', fishin', – gobble'm up, gobble'm up.
He talk: 'Yakai! Old Jabiroo, my friend, gooday!'
Jabiroo don't talk nothing. He just go gobble'm, gobble'm.
He don't talk properly: 'Yakai, my friend *Moolarli*, my mate.
You come now, must be hungry, you tuck out fish, we split'm'.
No, 'im don't talk nothing. Just go on tuck in, gobble'm up,
gobble'm up.

Well *Moolarli* know that not properly way, blackfella law.
Man can't fill'm up own stomach, 'nother fella go hungry.
Man got to think about 'nother fella first time. *Moolarli* talk:
'I teach this Jabiroo lesson. He got to learn sometime!
All right – you know Moolarli got that spear – that lightning?
Well, he pick'm up and he chuck'm – wheew! crackin' like thunder
and that range behind billabong come tumble down, make way for gorge
for river and he talk: 'Come on you fish, turtle, everysing,
you can go now, you free. That Jabiroo fella can't catch you,
you can swim away now down to salt water coast country'.
Then he talk along salt water crocodile: 'You can come up now,
camp on river, sleep in that shade place along paperbark'.
My people reckon we can't play round with country.
Only spirit can make him. That dangerous business.

Well, whiteman got different way from blackfella. He reckon:
'No, we don't want spirit. We got *ingineer*. Clever fella properly.
We got plenty man, tomahawk, truck, tractor, dynamite.
WHOOSH! We seen that big smoke come up. Everysing –
ground, tree, rock, shake like the finish coming.
Bird sing out – Carrr! Carrr! Carrr! Cattle, horse, kangaroo,
fright – gallop, gallop, nobody can't stop 'em.
By'n'bye, when 'im settle down – no more mountain that side –
no more goanna dreaming place. All that finish'.

* yes

Well, *Moolarli* got only *one spear* when he make that gorge first time.
He push that storm water down long way, away along coast.
He don't want to drown my country - (my born country).
Before, when I catch a fish, I cook 'em straight away,
I call my family: 'You come now! We got good tucker!'
Only now, today, when I take away hook I don't hurt 'im.
He go 'flap-flap' in my hand and I talk this way:

'You go back up there, that old station—Argyle station*—
(poor fella my old boss, my old missus. Nothing left that house
where I sweep'm every day!) You look out that house - you look out
windmill, tank, garden, kitchen, saddle shed.
You look out that store, that camp down there along crossing.
You look out that horse paddock, yard, mustering camp everywhere,
plain country ranges. You look out that limestone pocket
where I come from my mummy - that place where I lie along coolimon.
(Poor fella my old mummy, pass away long time ago).
You tell him, my country - *me*, old Maggie, old *Jilligan* -
she can't forget 'im, my country, she all day heart-crying.
You tell my country that secret. You tell him old Maggie,
old *Numbagina* woman belong *Mirriwung* - *she got that dream*.
You tell him *hang on!* Old *Jilligan* see what going happen
long time, might be close up, might be fifty, t'ousand year.
I think them old spirit fellows gone fast asleep'.

Well, one day him going wake up again . . . *Bilbilji*, that grasshopper,
that locust, he wake up on top that high place, that mountain,
and you hear'm wing like long time ago, make: Brrr! Brrr! Brrr!
And *Yarralong*, that snake fella (look out all-about
piccaninny spirit) he get fed up too much water.
He stretch himself - ough! ough! ough! then he jump up rainbow,
storm clouds come coming, big, high, everywhere,
thunder hard-talking all around sky.
Then *Moolarli* come along in whirlwind like helicopter,
pick up him spear, that lightning and WHEEW! straight through
that wall, that top-dam place - WHOOSH! like dynamite.
All that flood water go jump through Kangaroo Pocket,

* The Durack Station, Argyle, was also the traditional home of Maggie's
people. It was later flooded by the Ord River Scheme.

Down that dingo dreaming place, way down past Lomargin,
Push down that water-trap, that bridge close up Bandicoot,
Ivanhoe crossing, *Djigamurri*, *Bullgoomurri*, that Carlton country –
Swoosh down, lose'm in that big salt water.
And that the finish all that *ingineer* business.
Old Maggie, old *Jilligan*, she tell that fish:

'You bring this message my country, down there underneath.
You tell him *hold on*! Some day that dream coming true –
then he can stretch out and dry himself, my country.
He can breathe that air, he can open him up eye.
Bye'n'bye the grass come back again, tree, spinifex,
all them lizard and snake and wallaby, bandicoot, porcupine,
flying fox – all that good bush tucker – everysing come back.
And bird too – big mob brolga – dance like that –
and Jabiroo, emu, cockatoo – poor fella – I watch'm
flyin' over, lookin' down – Carrr! Carrr! What all that water?
What happen this good country? (That born place, my country.)
Little fish, you tell him – *me*, old Maggie, old *Jilligan*
heart-crying my born country. I got him here –
inside my heart, can't lose'm. I got that dream,
that message. You talk my country: Hold on!
Some time you gonna look out that sun again. You gonna
find all that moon and star. You gonna feel that warm wind blowing.
You gonna look-out that sky!'

JUDITH WRIGHT

At a Poetry Conference, Expo '67

This was the dream that woke me
from nembutal sleep into the pains of grief.

I had no hemisphere, yet all four hemispheres
reeled in a number-neoned sky,
over the grieved and starving, over the wars,
over the counter-clicking business corporations.
And round the cliffs of one grey vertical
squares of uncurtained light
showed all the sad, the human ends of love –
not springtime fulltime love but one-night stands
paid for with juke-box coins. And Sarah Vaughan was singing:
'Mist,' she sang,
but it was chemical mist
mist from incinerators for the dead,
mist from the dollar-mints and automobiles,
mist from the cities grown
from crystallizing chemicals.

To keep the crowds amused
they calmed them with the curves of lovely fireworks,
each arc exact, prefigured and agreed-on
by chemists and by weapon-builders.

Each in their planned and floodlit window-spaces
the poets stood and beckoned to the crowds.
'Language!' they cried with their wild human breath,
but in the squares beneath the crowds cried 'Numbers!'
'Words,' cried the poets from their past, 'Fires! Forests!'
the chemical greens of plastic leaves behind them.

'Rockets!' the crowds cried. 'Wars!'
and every window opened, every poet
began to burn with napalm flames.
and fires detached and fell into the crowds,
fires of a human flesh.

Here a hand fell, opening like a flower,
a firework breast, a glowing genital.

In every mirror-surface of the windows
poets blazed self-reflected
until their hearts at last burned best of all.

But here no woman rescued hearts to carry home
in cherished caskets. Over the squares below
only the flower-children lifted faces
that called out 'Pretty! Pretty!'
under the metronomed invisible stars.

You might have thought the flames that fell among them
would light the crowds and scar them to the bone,
but it was only language burning. Only
incinerated words. Few phrases
did more than hang above the crowds
an unaccepted holy ghost, a word
that no one dared to take and speak.

Then the squares darkened and the lifted faces
went grey with ash.

The show is over, cried the amplifiers.
Take home your souvenirs. Those burned-out sticks
are radio-active, ticking like geiger counters,
the spinal cords of poets, bright medullas
and clever cortexes. Hang them on your walls.
They'll do to mark your time.

Midnight is closing-time.
The crowds went drifting
into the metro. Only a few
carried their midnight souvenirs, their burned-out rockets.
The metro doors all closed.

Now under midnight's sign
there's nothing but the dark, the nembutal sleep,
the hemispheres are flattened like Mercator
projections; folded like fans.
The sweepers issue from their corners
and that show's over.

Stillborn

Those who have once admitted
within their pulse and blood
the chill of that most loving
that most despairing child
known what is never told –
the arctic anti-god,
the secret of the cold.

Those who have once expected
the pains of that dark birth
which takes but without giving
and ends in double loss –
they still reach hands across
to grave from flowering earth,
to shroud from living dress.

Alive, they should be dead
who cheated their own death,
and I have heard them cry
when all else was lying still
'O that I stand above
while you lie down beneath!'
Such women weep for love
of one who drew no breath
and in the night they lie
giving the breast to death.

Letter

How write an honest letter
to you, my dearest?
We know each other well –
not well enough.

You, the dark baby hung
in a nurse's arms,
seen through a mist – your eyes
still vague, a stranger's eyes;

hung in a hospital world
of drugs and fevers.
You, too much wanted,
reared in betraying love.

Yes, love is dangerous.
The innocent beginner
can take for crystal-true
that rainbow surface;

surprise, surprise –
paddling the slime-dark bottom
the bull-rout's sting and spine
stuns your soft foot.

Why try to give
what never can be given –
safety, a green world?
It's mined, the trip-wire's waiting.

Perhaps we should have trained you
in using weapons,
bequeathed you a straight eye,
a sure-shot trigger-finger,

or that most commonplace
of self-defences,
an eye to Number One,
shop-lifting skills,

a fibrous heart, a head
sharp with arithmetic
to figure out the chances?
You'd not have that on.

What then? Drop-out, dry-rot?
Wipe all the questions
into an easy haze,
a fix for everything?

Or split the mind apart –
an old solution –
shouting to mental-nurses
your coded secrets?

I promised you unborn
something better than that –
the chance of love; clarity,
charity, caritas – dearest,

don't throw it in. Keep searching.
Dance even among these
poisoned swords; frightened only
of not being what you are –

of not expecting love
or hoping truth;
of sitting in lost corners
ill-willing time.

I promised what's not given,
and should repent of that,
but do not. You are you,
finding your own way;

nothing to do with me,
though all I care for.
I blow a kiss on paper.
I send your letter.

Report of a Working-Party

Ladies and gentlemen, we have returned
from our foray into the future.
Our report is appended.

The final peaks are impossibly steep.
It took us all our mathematics
to climb those exponential slopes.
We finally had to turn back
because we were starting too many avalanches.
We feared for your safety below.

Frankly we don't think you'll ever make the top.
Hidden by cloud (or smog) we were unable to see it;
there's vertigo in those verticals.
So we identified a certain ceiling
beyond which we consider settlement will be impossible.

Indeed, even at that height
our instruments detected certain warning-signals,
a lack of breathable air, a scarcity
of organisms other than ourselves;
so far above the tree-line
only certain insects appear to survive.

Apart from that, we were saddened
by the loss of some members of the working-party.
Our zoologist apparently was unable
to adapt to the height we reached.
We regret that he cut the rope.

About the Advance Party's fate we are uncertain.
It included, as you know, our economist,
the Chaplain, and the official representative
of the Government, Mr John Simple.
They were attempting to hack out a plateau
for the tents.
That incident started the avalanches.

Ladies and gentlemen, we are aware
our report must be a disappointment,
but we recommend you do not proceed.

Ladies and gentlemen . . .

Ladies and gentlemen!

The Trap

'I love you,' said the child,
but the parrot with its blazing breast and wing
flaunted in the high tree, love's very beckoning,
and would not be beguiled.

Look how first innocence
darkens through shades of knowledge and desire!
 – the bait, the trap, the patience! When the wire
snaps shut, his eyes' triumphant insolence!

'I loved it and it would not come to me.'
Now love is gone.
Cunning and will undo us. We must be
their prisoners, boy, and in a bitterer cage
endure their lifelong rage.
Look round you. See, the chains on everyone.

Quick, save yourself! Undo
that door and let him go.

Eve to Her Daughters

It was not I who began it.
Turned out into draughty caves,
hungry so often, having to work for our bread,
hearing the children whining,
I was nevertheless not unhappy.
Where Adam went I was fairly contented to go.
I adapted myself to the punishment: it was my life.

But Adam, you know . . .!
He kept on brooding over the insult,
over the trick They had played on us, over the scolding.
He had discovered a flaw in himself
and he had to make up for it.

Outside Eden the earth was imperfect,
the seasons changed, the game was fleet-footed,
he had to work for our living, and he didn't like it.
He even complained of my cooking
(it was hard to compete with Heaven).

So he set to work.
The earth must be made a new Eden
with central heating, domesticated animals,
mechanical harvesters, combustion engines,
escalators, refrigerators,
and modern means of communication
and multiplied opportunities for safe investment
and higher education for Abel and Cain
and the rest of the family.
You can see how his pride had been hurt.

In the process he had to unravel everything,
because he believed that mechanism
was the whole secret – he was always mechanical-minded.
He got to the very inside of the whole machine
exclaiming as he went, So this is how it works!
And now that I know how it works, why, I must have invented it.
As for God and the Other, they cannot be demonstrated,

and what cannot be demonstrated
doesn't exist.
You see, he had always been jealous.

Yes, he got to the centre
where nothing at all can be demonstrated.
And clearly he doesn't exist; but he refuses
to accept the conclusion.
You see, he was always an egotist.

It was warmer than this in the cave;
there was none of this fall-out.
I would suggest, for the sake of the children,
that it's time you took over.

But you are my daughters, you inherit my own faults of character;
you are submissive, following Adam
even beyond existence.
Faults of character have their own logic
and it always works out.
I observed this with Abel and Cain.

Perhaps the whole elaborate fable
right from the beginning
is meant to demonstrate this; perhaps it's the whole secret.
Perhaps nothing exists but our faults?
At least they can be demonstrated.

But it's useless to make
such a suggestion to Adam.
He has turned himself into God,
who is faultless, and doesn't exist.

Halfway

I saw a tadpole once in a sheet of ice
(a freakish joke played by my country's weather).
He hung at arrest, displayed as it were in glass,
an illustration of neither one thing nor the other.

His head was a frog's, and his hinder legs had grown
ready to climb and jump to his promised land;
but his bladed tail in the ice-pane weighed him down.
He seemed to accost my eye with his budding hand.

'I am neither one thing nor the other, not here nor there.
I saw great lights in the place where I would be,
but rose too soon, half made for water, half air,
and they have gripped and stilled and enchanted me.

'Is that world real, or a dream I cannot reach?
Beneath me the dark familiar waters flow
and my fellows huddle and nuzzle each to each,
while motionless here I stare where I cannot go.'

The comic O of his mouth, his gold-rimmed eyes,
looked in that lustrous glaze as though they'd ask
my vague divinity, looming in stooped surprise,
for death or rescue. But neither was my task.

Waking halfway from a dream one winter night
I remembered him as a poem I had to write.

DOROTHY AUCHTERLONIE

A Problem of Language

How praise a man? She cannot vow
His lips are red, his brow is snow,
Nor celebrate a smooth white breast
While gazing on his hairy chest;
And though a well-turned leg might please,
More often he has knobbly knees;
His hair excites no rapt attention –
If there's enough of it to mention.
She cannot praise his damask skin,
Still less the suit he's wrapped it in;
And even if he's like Apollo
To gaze upon, it does not follow
That she may specify the features
That mark him off from other creatures.
No rime can hymn her great occasion
But by a process of evasion;
And so she gives the problem over,
Describes her love, but not her lover,
Despairs of words to tell us that
Her heart sings his magnificat.

Present Tense

'Nothing can ever come of it,' he said.
 – Outside the window, the white rose waved its head,
A late bird sang, insouciant, in the tree,
The sunset stained the river red.

'There is no future, none at all,' he said.
 – She stretched her arms up from the tumbled bed:
'What future has the river or the rose?' said she,
'The bird's song is, and nothing comes of red.'

He held her as the river holds the red
Stain of sunset; as, when the bird has fled,
The tree holds the song. 'Listen,' said she,
'Bird, rose and sunlit water sing from this bed.'

NANCY CATO

Mallee Farmer

You planted wheat and you reaped white gibbers
You ran some sheep but the crows were robbers
Of eyes and entrails and even the wool,
Plucked from the carcass before it was cool.

You cleared the mallee and sand blew over
Fence and road to the slow green river,
You prayed for rain but the sky breathed dust
Of long-dead farmers and the soil's red rust.

You ploughed up the paddocks with a stump-jump plough,
But the gates were open and the drought walked through:
Now the old house crumbles and bares its bones
And the land is left to the crows and the stones.

Day's End

Day's ending had enough beauty without this,
The full moon rising slow in honeyed light:
Fantastic suns that set in separate globes
Through bands of distorting cloud, as streamers, lanterns,
Lozenges orange and red; and a pure sky
Distilled to luminous green. Where the dripping tap
Has made a shallow pool for the thirsty birds,
I lean on the rusted railing and idly stare
Across the vineyard's waveless sea of leaves
At diamonds pricking out along the rim
Of the wide plain, and, two-dimensional,
The cardboard city floating in the air.

MADGE STAUNTON

from Writers and War

In Memory of Dietrick Bonhoeffer
(Day Lilies)

How could she know as she dug
the plot to lay the tubers
in, their quick eyes to the light,
she would cut them when they stood
 – their buds so full of promise –
and carry them to break and
star the prison of her son.

Locked within the fortress walls
he saw, each day, the lilies
bloom and in a world at war
watched each night from his darkened
cell giant, elongated pods
seeding Berlin. Seeds that burst
immediate, monstrous flowers.

He was hanged at Flossenburg.
How could he know behind dead
eyes, as they cut him down and
dug the plot to lay him in,
his writings – leaves so filled with
promise – would unfold to bloom
and star prisons of the mind.

ANNE ELDER

Crazy Woman

On the first day of autumn Euterpe called to me:
I am the Muse that sits musing under the lyric tree
plucking and plaiting the thoughtful branches
deep in the heart of the public gardens
where I first saw you, a queer child with your grandfather.
It is nice here, you should be with me.
We can sit alone.
I will pluck you and suck you the fruit for a serious poem.

So I went, and sure enough it was nice;
the first leaf already fallen,
the last white daisy still crawling
in bluish dewy grass, a pair of birds
black-white and neat, no longer matey, but still friendly,
unsurprised at my feet.
But another madwoman came by
and pecked me with her smile. Aren't they tame
she said, Yes I said, What's their name
she said, A couple called Magpie Lark I said,
built last spring, now semi-detached, it's autumn,
and she said fancy, what a shame.

I detached myself to the perfect seclusion
of the remembered grotto, the only intrusion
a fountaining cherubic boy, his little bronze spout
of Eros still delightful as when my grandfather
took pains not to point it out.
But a chap came by who was foreign.
You are zitting in vot beautiful zun, he said,
yes I said abstractedly (I was writing a serious poem)
and he went and sat tactfully
on the next seat. How lonely can you get
to be looking so slantingly
at my withering crossed knee.

For security I became engaged to the gardener
in passionately horticultural conversation
of considerable duration,
even to how the nights in the gardens of Spain
are enlivened with runnels and babbles
of conversational water, and he agreed with me
that the Spanish are gardeners of great subtlety
What's that, I said, like a fern dotted with stars?
Oh that, that's a thing we've had for years
for which no municipal gardener cares,
but if you would like it, come into the shrubbery
and I will give you a good root
he said, with subtlety I thought,
and I jumped at it
and went off with my fern dripping good fruitful earth
down the mysterious path.

But along the misty vistas of Arcady
behold young lovers approaching, she
not beautiful but beautifully shy,
he with the true, the demented languishing eye,
swinging along wonderfully lonely
hand in hand worlds apart
by the width of the path
so that I met them where they joined, they dropped hands
for the Weird Woman gathering ferns and simples
and muttering God keep you under her breath
like a gipsy, meaning no harm.

I debated how to say it aloud,
to their alarm. Before our death
there is much to communicate that goes by the board
because it is thought unusual indeed crazy
to gather the fallen leaf and the daisy,
the magpie lark and the private lark
in the public park,
the eternal cherubic spout, the nakedness
and lovingness of loneliness
into the right word
to bless our other selves in the name of the Lord.

With coupled hands and crooked stare
and pointed smile they dance around
the poor old crazy head-in-air,
the poet, who has first to find
the spangled fern, the gift, then grow it
bedded in the heart's ground.

Seen Out

Some of them evil, most good,
all nice people with various eyes.
They are The Club.

The band has packed, the white cloths discreetly
being flapped and the dregs of the bubbly
drained in kitchens. The smoke
has been forced with the gaiety
up to the lofty ceiling; but some still sit
masticating the last rags of conversation.
The fine brain bends to its neighbouring dome, a frontal
obeisance as though to the Privy Council, sharing
dignity, reminiscence, a witticism
desiccated, deprecated. The beloved obstetrician
off duty is quacking softly
to an ex-victim. A shimmer, a trailed fur
looms in the archway, beckoning with a nose.
'Time, gentlemen, please . . . delightful . . . past our bed . . .'

In the hall they sort into a graceful procession,
here with a bluff arm or a blurry pleasantry,
here with the slightly inhibited belch of weary lechery,
there with even a touch of accustomed hands
as though in a decorous round-dance they have not needed
to rehearse for the last decade. Out into the night
through cedar portals they sway themselves.
The beautiful young wives, a little roguish and elated,
drop names, smoothing the satin laps of their success.
The great bosom beneath a purple coiffure
sinks with a constrained sigh into the front seat,
murmuring 'Shall I drive, dear?' Dear grunts.

NANCY GORDON

The Night She Explored Her Psyche

You must you know explore your psyche –
he offered her a cigarette.
Oh so correct spectacles
behind the polished desk
with the kleenex and her file
which he started to read on the hour
came to the door at five past
showed her in with the small chat to get her started.

She sat
Mummie had drilled her well
skirt pulled over her knees.
When the strings were pulled
she danced.
At twenty-five past the hour
he showed her out
she hadn't finished the cigarette.

That night
she took her psyche
into the hot still moonlit air
and the scent of the datura.
Then clear like a bell
moonlight awake
the wagtail called.
It went in like a probe
her psyche she found
was spun sugar.
Mother father brother
embedded like plums.
She put in a thumb
and ate them.

KATH WALKER

No More Boomerang

No more boomerang
No more spear;
Now all civilized –
Colour bar and beer.

No more corroboree,
Gay dance and din.
Now we got movies,
And pay to go in.

No more sharing
What the hunter brings.
Now we work for money,
Then pay it back for things.

Now we track bosses
To catch a few bob,
Now we go walkabout
On bus to the job.

One time naked,
Who never knew shame;
Now we put clothes on
To hide whatsaname.

No more gunya,
Now bungalow,
Paid by hire purchase
In twenty year or so.

Lay down the stone axe,
Take up the steel,
And work like a nigger
For a white man meal.

No more firesticks
That made the whites scoff.
Now all electric,
And no better off.

Bunyip he finish,
Now got instead
White fella Bunyip,
Call him Red.

Abstract picture now –
What they coming at?
Cripes, in our caves we
Did better than that.

Black hunted wallaby,
White hunt dollar;
White fella witch-doctor
Wear dog-collar.

No more message-stick;
Lubras and lads
Got television now,
Mostly ads.

Lay down the woomera,
Lay down the waddy.
Now we got atom-bomb,
End *every*body.

Gifts

'I will bring you love,' said the young lover,
'A glad light to dance in your dark eye.
Pendants I will bring of the white bone,
And gay parrot feathers to deck your hair.'

But she only shook her head.

'I will put a child in your arms,' he said,
'Will be a great headman, great rain-maker.
I will make remembered songs about you
That all the tribes in all the wandering camps
Will sing for ever.'

But she was not impressed.

'I will bring you the still moonlight on the lagoon,
And steal for you the singing of all the birds;
I will bring down the stars of heaven to you,
And put the bright rainbow into your hand.'

'No,' she said, 'bring me tree-grubs.'

We are Going

For Grannie Coolwell

They came in to the little town
A semi-naked band subdued and silent,
All that remained of their tribe.
They came here to the place of their old bora ground
Where now the many white men hurry about like ants.
Notice of estate agent reads: 'Rubbish May Be Tipped Here'.
Now it half covers the traces of the old bora ring.
They sit and are confused, they cannot say their thoughts:
'We are as strangers here now, but the white tribe are the strangers.
We belong here, we are of the old ways.
We are the corroboree and the bora ground,
We are the old sacred ceremonies, the laws of the elders.
We are the wonder tales of Dream Time, the tribal legends told.
We are the past, the hunts and the laughing games, the wandering
    camp fires.
We are the lightning-bolt over Gaphembah Hill
Quick and terrible,
And the Thunder after him, that loud fellow.
We are the quiet daybreak paling the dark lagoon.
We are the shadow-ghosts creeping back as the camp fires burn low.
We are nature and the past, all the old ways
Gone now and scattered.
The scrubs are gone, the hunting and the laughter.
The eagle is gone, the emu and the kangaroo are gone from this place.
The bora ring is gone.
The corroboree is gone.
And we are going.'

Ballad of the Totems

My father was Noonuccal man and kept old tribal way,
His totem was the Carpet Snake, whom none must ever slay;
But mother was of Peewee clan, and loudly she expressed
The daring view that carpet snakes were nothing but a pest.

Now one lived right inside with us in full immunity,
For no one dared to interfere with father's stern decree:
A mighty fellow ten feet long, and as we lay in bed
We kids could watch him round a beam not far above our head.

Only the dog was scared of him, we'd hear its whines and growls,
But mother fiercely hated him because he took her fowls.
You should have heard her diatribes that flowed in angry torrents
With words you never see in print, except in D. H. Lawrence.

'I kill that robber,' she would scream, fierce as a spotted cat;
'You see that bulge inside of him? My speckly hen make that!'
But father's loud and strict command made even mother quake;
I think he'd sooner kill a man than kill a carpet snake.

That reptile was a greedy-guts, and as each bulge digested
He'd come down on the hunt at night as appetite suggested.
We heard his stealthy slithering sound across the earthen floor,
While the dog gave a startled yelp and bolted out the door.

Then over in the chicken-yard hysterical fowls gave tongue,
Loud frantic squawks accompanied by the barking of the mung,
Until at last the racket passed, and then to solve the riddle,
Next morning he was back up there with a new bulge in his middle.

When father died we wailed and cried, our grief was deep and sore,
And strange to say from that sad day the snake was seen no more.
The wise old men explained to us: 'It was his tribal brother,
And that is why it done a guy' – but some looked hard at mother.

She seemed to have a secret smile, her eyes were smug and wary,
She looked as innocent as the cat that ate the pet canary.
We never knew, but anyhow (to end this tragic rhyme)
I think we all had snake for tea one day about that time.

ROSEMARY DOBSON

Good Friday, Boston

After all my travelling I think this:
Looked at from the sky cities are orderly
Prove the straight inheritance from the Roman.
Bridges hang from compass-lines,
Buildings are boxed, cars slotted into car-parks.

But amongst and below them, the muddle:
Feet stumble, sleeve-ends catch, cinders
Fret at the eyelid. Turnstiles deceive us
Impartially, leaving and entering,
And the noise, the askance-ness!

Strange then to come up from below to Boston Common
To the Quakers standing in snow like straight lead pencils
Each marking a line on the snow – a declaration.
Each saying No to violence and Yes to peace.
In silence. Not moving.

The Eye

One day the dark fell over my eye.
It was like a blind drawn halfway down
A holland blind, dense, a sheet of shadow.
Afterwards it frayed and dipped at the edges
Filaments thinned and broke away, drifting –
Seemed to be birds with the motion of swimmers.
I think of last year as the year of the clouds.
Great cumulus gathered at morning gravely
Circling the world in contemplation,
At noon dispersed, at evening gathered
Again in council. The filaments moving
Seemed dark birds against their whiteness
Or drifting, undeciphered omens.
With the palm of my hand I cover my eye,
Cover, uncover. They are always there.

Child with a Cockatoo

Portrait of Anne, daughter of the Earl of Bedford,
by S. Verelst

'Paid by my lord, one portrait, Lady Anne,
Full length with bird and landscape, twenty pounds
And framed withal. I say received. Verelst.'

So signed the painter, bowed, and took his leave.
My Lady Anne smiled in the gallery
A small, grave child, dark-eyed, half turned to show
Her five bare toes beneath the garment's hem,
In stormy landscape with a swirl of drapes.
And, who knows why, perhaps my lady wept
To stand so long and watch the painter's brush
Flicker between the palette and the cloth
While from the sun-drenched orchard all the day
She heard her sisters calling each to each.
And someone gave, to drive the tears away,
That sulphur-crested bird with great white wings,
The wise, harsh bird – as old and wise as Time
Whose well-dark eyes the wonder kept and closed.
So many years to come and still, he knew,
Brooded that great, dark island continent
Terra Australis.

                    To those fabled shores
Not William Dampier, pirating for gold,
Nor Captain Cook his westward course had set
Jumped from the longboat, waded through the surf,
And clapt his flag ashore at Botany Bay.
Terra Australis, unimagined land –
Only that sulphur-crested bird could tell
Of dark men moving silently through trees,
Of stones and silent dawns, of blackened earth
And the long golden blaze of afternoon.
That vagrant which an ear-ringed sailor caught
(Dropped from the sky, near dead, far out to sea)
And caged and kept, till, landing at the docks,
Walked whistling up the Strand and sold it then,
The curious bird, its cynic eyes half-closed,
To the Duke's steward, drunken at an inn.

And he lived on, the old adventurer,
And kept his counsel, was a sign unread,
A disregarded prologue to an age.
So one might find a meteor from the sun
Or sound one trumpet ere the play's begun.

Captain Svenson

Lying in the hospital I heard the white-veiled sisters neigh,
Tossing their veils like fillies, stepping high

On the long bright shiny floors. Oh, I heard them
  whinny and say –

Captain Svenson will be admitted Monday,
Captain Svenson has rung to know
Does his room have a view of the harbour,
Can he listen to the radio?
The yacht-race starts on Wednesday morning –
Oh, and Sister, Sister, Sister,
The Mariners' League is on the phone,
When is the Captain's operation?
Tell them Tuesday, early in the morning.
And I thought: has he strayed from a Slessor poem?

The white-maned sisters prance like fillies
On neat white hooves from room to room
With trays, thermometers, letters, flowers,
Sharp, sharp scissors and cotton wool.
Limp as a drowned man down in the theatre
The Captain lies where he'd rather not be.
Someone listens to his ticking heart-beats:
The surgeon is snipping: one, two, three.
Back in a trice on a trolley goes the Captain,
Back to his room with a wink of the sea.

I lie on my bed and I think of the Captain
While the sisters whinny outside my door,

Their white manes tossing like waves of the sea.
Do waves of pain wash over you, Captain,
And do you fear you are like to die?
Sister! What of Captain Svenson?

Kindly give the message that Captain Svenson
Passed a comfortable night, and is now as well –
As well, that is, as can be expected.
He holds a telescope up to the window
And rolls an eye as blue as the sea.
When I took his pulse a moment ago,
Sister, Sister, how he looked at me!
Oh Sister, Sister. Oh, Sister, Oh!

The Nightmare

for C.S.*

I sit beside the bed where she lies dreaming
Of pyrrhic victories and sharp words said,
She will annihilate the hospital

She will destroy the medical profession
And, kicking her feet free, walk into the world.
She moves her fist to her mouth as a child does.

Suppose her smouldering thoughts break out in flame
Not to consume bed, nightdress, flesh and hair
But the mind, the working and the making mind

That built those towers which the world applauds,
And leave upon the bed this breathing body
Scarred with the rage and trouble of her time?

I have dreamt her nightmare for her. She wakes up
And turns to smile with quick complicity,
'I wasn't asleep. I watched you sitting there.'

* C.S. – the novelist, Christina Stead. *eds*

GWEN HARWOOD

An Address to My Muse

Dear Sir, or Madam, as the case is,
blest being of so many faces,
known to the Furies and the Graces,
   don't be a clown,
just slip off those artistic braces
   and settle down.

Please put off all your other suitors,
the ponces and the lusty rooters,
the plagiarists and sneaky looters –
   or break their necks –
unload that party of freebooters.
   Show me your sex.

How often I've sat late at night
wrestling to get my verses right
and asked you for a little light,
   'Mehr Licht,' like Goethe.
You've left me, you hermaphrodite,
   to drink with Kröte.

Sir, Madam, when the wine is known,
the woman's drunk; I'm on my own;
your silence cuts me to the bone.
   Am I a freak?
Squeeze something from that heart of stone,
   in mercy, speak!

Male colleagues making open mention
of how they're spared the fearful tension
of playing the two-part invention
   which I must learn,
would never touch the metric pension
   I have to earn.

Madam, or Sir, why so aloof?
I shouldn't have to offer proof

that we live under the same roof.
    – What, are you going?
Pegasus set, with stamping hoof,
    Hippocrene flowing.

Surely a spring where all may drink
and turn black sorrows into ink.
Or is that true and blushful pink
    water restricted?
If it's for men alone, I think
    I'll be convicted.

O Muse, Sir, Madam of renown,
take off that multicoloured gown,
remove the mask, wipe off the frown,
    we'll name no names.
Just watch the world, when we lie down,
    go up in flames.

Night Thoughts: Baby & Demon

Baby I'm sick. I need
nursing. Give me your breast.
My orifices bleed.
I cannot sleep. My chest
shakes like a window. Light
guts me. My head's not right.

Demon, we're old, old chap.
Born under the same sign
after some classic rape.
Gemini. Yours is mine.
Sickness and health. We'll share
the end of this affair.

Baby, I'm sick to death.
But I can't die. You do
the songs, you've got the breath.

Give them the old soft shoe.
Put on a lovely show.
Put on your wig, and go.

The service station flags, denticulate
plastic, snap in the wind. Hunched seabirds wait

for light to quench the unmeaning lights of town.
This day will bring the fabulous summer down.

Weather no memory can match will fade
to memory, leaf-drift in the pines' thick shade.

All night salt water stroked and shaped the sand.
All night I heard it. Your bravura hand

chimed me to shores beyond time's rocking swell.
The last cars leave the shabby beach motel.

Lovers and drunks unroofed in sobering air
disperse, ghost-coloured in the streetlight-glare.

   Rock-a-bye Baby
     in the motel
   Baby will kiss
     and Demon will tell.

One candle lights us. Night's cool airs begin
to lick the luminous edges of our skin.

   When the bough bends
     the apple will fall
   Baby knows nothing
     Demon knows all.

Draw up the voluptuously crumpled sheet.
In rose-dark silence gentle tongues repeat
the body's triumph through its grand eclipse.
I feel your pulsebeat through my fingertips.

   Baby's a rocker
     lost on the shore.
   Demon's a mocker.
     Baby's a whore.

World of the happy, innocent and whole:
the body's the best picture of the soul
couched like an animal in savage grace.
Ghost after ghost obscures your sleeping face.

My baby's like a bird of day
    that flutters from my side,
my baby's like an empty beach
    that's ravished by the tide.

So fair are you, my bonny lass,
    so sick and strange am I,
that I must lie with all your loves
    and suck your sweetness dry.

And drink your juices dry, my dear,
    and grind your bones to sand,
then I will walk the empty shore
    and sift you through my hand.

And sift you through my hand, my dear,
    and find you grain by grain,
and build your body bone by bone
    and flesh those bones again,

with flesh from all your loves, my love,
    while tides and seasons stream,
until you wake by candle-light
    from your midsummer dream,

and like some gentle creature meet
    the huntsman's murderous eye,
and know you never shall escape
    however fast you fly.

Unhoused I'll shout my drunken songs
    and through the streets I'll go
compelling all I meet to toast
    the bride they do not know.

Till all your tears are dry, my love,
    and your ghosts fade in the sun.
Be sure I'll have your heart, my love,
    when all your loving's done.

'I am the Captain of my Soul'

The human body is the best picture of the human soul.
                              – LUDWIG WITTGENSTEIN

But the Captain is drunk, and the crew
hauling hard on his windlass of fury are whipped
by his know-nothing rage. Their terror
troubles the sunlight. 'Now tell me,'
the Captain says, as his drunkenness
drifts into tears, 'what's to keep me
at ease in this harbour?'
                              'We'll tell you,'
say Hands, 'in our headlong chase through a fugue

for three voices, you heard a fourth voice naming
divisions of silence. We'll summon
that voice once again, it may tell you
of marvels wrung from sorrow endured.'
'We have seen,' say Eyes, 'how in Venice
the steps of churches open and close
like marble fans under water.'

'You can rot in your sockets,' the Captain cries.

'I have children,' says Body, haloed
in tenderness, firm in ripeness still.
'I grew gross with their stress, I went spinning
in a vortex of pain. I gave my breast
and its beauty to nourish their heedless growth.
They jump on my shadow in mischievous joy.
On their lives your astonishing sorrows
flow easy as water on marble steps.'

'Lass sie betteln gehn,' roars the Captain
as his old wounds burn, and he gulps
from his flagon of grief. 'You servants, you things,
stand up there! *You* with the ageing choir-boy face,
and *you* with your facile dexterity, *you*
with your marble hallucinations, COME!'

Hands, eyes, body keel to the void as the drunken
Captain sings in his wilderness of water.

Carnal Knowledge II

Grasshoppers click and whirr.
Stones grow in the field.
Autumnal warmth is sealed
in a gold skin of light
on darkness plunging down
to earth's black molten core.

Earth has no more to yield.
Her blond grasses are dry.
  Nestling my cheek against
  the hollow of your thigh
  I lay cockeyed with love
  in the most literal sense.

Your eyes, kingfisher blue.
This was the season, this
the light, the halcyon air.
Our window framed this place.
If there were music here,
insectile, abstract, bare,

it would bless no human ear.
Shadows lie with the stones.
Bury our hearts, perhaps
they'll strike it rich in earth's
black marrow, crack, take root,
bring forth vines, blossom, fruit.

  Roses knocked on the glass.
  Wine like a running stream
  no evil spell could cross
  flowed round the house of touch.
God grant me drunkenness
if this is sober knowledge,

song to melt sea and sky
apart, and lift these hills
from the shadow of what was,
and roll them back, and lie
in naked ignorance
in the hollow of your thigh.

Suburban Sonnet: Boxing Day

Gold, silver, pink and blue, the globes distort her,
framed in the doorway: woman with a broom.
Wrappings and toys lie scattered round the room.
A glossy magazine the children bought her
lies open: *How to keep your husband's love.*
She stands and stares, as if in recollection,
at her own staring acid-pink reflection.
The simple fact is, she's too tired to move.

O where's the demon lover, the wild boy
who kissed the future to her flesh beneath
what skies, what stars, what space! and swore to love her
through hell's own fires? A child stretches above her
and, laughing, crowns her with a tinsel wreath.
She gathers up a new, dismembered toy.

Mid-Channel

'The days shall come upon you, that he will take you away with hooks,
and your posterity with fishhooks.' – Amos, IV, 2.

Cod inert as an old boot,
tangling dance of the little shark,
perch-nibble, flathead-jerk –
blindfold I'd know them on my line.

Fugitive gleam on scale and fin,
lustrous eye, opalescent belly
dry and die in the undesired
element. A day will come,

matter-of-fact as knife and plate,
with death's hook in my jaw, and language
unspeakable, the line full out.
I'll tire you with my choking weight

old monster anchored in the void.
My God, you'll wonder what you've caught.
Land me in hell itself at last
I'll stab and swell your wounds with poison.

Not here, not now. Water's my kingdom
tonight, my line makes starspecks tremble.
The dinghy's decked with golden eyes
and still the cod boil round my bait.

NORA KROUK

I died yesterday on a Tel Aviv bus
and cannot relate to the person in
this cool home dusting, cleaning,
switching things on, turning on,
breathing and even loving: alive.

In hail of bullets I fell,
clutched at nothing, thought:
hot – dusty – sore.

No more – they had said –
no more of unwarranted dying
for being a Jew. So, just a few.

Suddenly plucked from a busy, full,
worrisome, warm life of high prices,
government follies, Sharon's temper,
Tirza's adventures, worries over
Mamma's arthritis and a new dress
for Yael I have died yesterday.
Shema Israel.

DOROTHY HEWETT

This Time

I

The rain falls, the wind
blows in the canyons of the University.
Drinking with the Professor of English
behind the plate-glass windows
the last crocus is whipped to death.

Heidelberg paraplegics; the boy dies in the iron lung,
his 21 kindly candles winking in the last light on the balcony;
the ice-caked windscreen fogs, the Flame of Remembrance
burns like hell-fire in the wintry air by the Psychiatric Clinic;
the light, like a faulty film, slips from my detached retina in the
    Eye Hospital.

Your house is a mausoleum, the springing lids
of Victorian jewel boxes click in the stillness,
the stuffed monkey swings in the cupboard behind your eyes.
The white terrace creaks in the wind;
I lie like a seed curled in the body of the house,
The footsteps troop up the stairs
and circle my bed to judge me.
I wrestle on the floor, in a harsh light,
                        with an old familiar angel,
our mutual friends give me a cheek to kiss.
Outside in the dark the magpies whistle;
at the foot of the stairs in the empty hall each evening
the kitten places my black fur glove like a clue.

II

It will soon be over.
I wrap myself in a black cloak
to hide with the English Department in the cafeteria,
but when you come towards me
my body husks and I cling to your hands.

I am too tired,
I will travel centuries of escalators to Richmond,
and think of you all night in Paddy's Market
                    amongst the refugees from Katmandu.
I sit with the Catholic poets;
(a relic of some dim Pre-Raphaelite girl)
they understand the nature of suffering,
and my times with you are all like
                    Stations of the Cross.
A night of Merka's dolls:
I discover them, imprisoned in paperweights,
moon faces float darkbeaked above the tide,
their fishtails flick with grief.
I will fly to Sydney, weeping like a dolphin.

III

In the garden, in the morning,
I was like Eve,
I was like sin in red velvet,
I walked barefoot
till my hem was wet, the globes spun
on the lemon trees your body's weight,
the sun came up, my children slept.
With my hands full of winter flowers
I enter my own house
and open the Art Exhibition.
As we drive home across the winter city,
the dark comes down with birds.
My words lash out like hail,
hunched over the wheel you don't protect yourself.
Lucky Untouchable! you are always guilty.
The airport swarms, some terminal in hell.
We swap quotations;
'And thus contending on the plains of Heaven;'
hands part, I'm on firm ground;
'With thee conversing I forget all time.'
Take me to Beechworth, cover me with kisses.
Where my great-neverending-grandmother served Ned Kelly,
I could be one of your green ladies.

You will never go in search of the woman you love,
casting her sacred pots in some London suburb.
I watch you walk away, incestuous twin,
miracle and monster, my other self.
A black swan floats, broken-necked in the Airport pool,
                    stoned by innocence.

Planes overhead:
I take to the freeway, driving fast and cold,
looking for a fix.
In the empty house the imprint of your head
on a leather chair; I strip the bed
and leaving, look back once.
Shut in my study I teach them 'Paradise Lost.'

IV

I've made it once again,
gone past the pitch of grief,
each time it's easier and nonchalant.
Slip into it Old Friend; a fatal treaty.
I stretch my limbs, knowing the stages
of withdrawal, irony contributes,
(but not much) it's giving yourself to pain,
no twilight sleep, cold turkey!
It helps to be a woman, not in God's image.
I weep in terminals and public libraries.

It's over now,
the waking up to pain,
the compensatory eating's almost stopped.
On a diet I'm even interested in other men.
My calendar measures months.
My capacity for faithfulness was always limited.
Yet there's a dreariness, not visionary at all,
old flicks, old times,
the sepia snapshots in my family album:
Watergate breaks
its stoney teeth and bridge of sighs
flying Old Glory, the wiretappers' lament.
Flesh fails,

my bones are stiff, yet winter passes,
spring builds its hopes.
I find the same face in the bathroom mirror.
Hard to sink back again to middle-age.

Now that the pain has gone
I'm lost without it,
no rhythm to my days, no sense of purpose;
brute force, a wheel to break on
balanced time, but that's all lost.
I turn your letters in a drawer,
and think of words I wrote,
know the old itch for permanence
made these sly icons of ephemera.
But here's the proof we lived
to write each other from our distant cities,
suffered alone in motel rooms,
put out a hand, smiled, sat up naked,
shared each other's bodies . . .
phoney libertines and beautiful fucks!

Somewhere in a far city the night comes down,
                    (two hours early)
sound waves crackle, you die in bed
of a broken heart, your hand reaching
                    for the telephone
before the blackness cuts the last receiver;
I would have answered one long distance call.
You lie with the Sisters of Mercy
under the dangling man,
your ribcage cracked,
your side open to their hands.
'Jesus! but that was close!'
'We prefer, my son, to call it the will of God.'
(We two non-believers, atheists to the end.)

I walk in the garden in the last light
and hear a bird call, but no soul sings out.
Your books are on my shelf, on the dust jackets
I trace your beardless face,

                    younger . . . more vulnerable . . .
The engaged signal beeps mournfully through the house.

Anniversary

Death is in the air –

today is the anniversary of his death in October
(he would have been thirty-one)
I went home to High Street
& couldn't feed the new baby
my milk had dried up
so I sat holding him numbly
looking for the soft spot on the top of his head
while they fed me three more librium
you're only crying for yourself he said
but I kept on saying *It's the waste I can't bear.*

All that winter we lived
in the longest street in the world
he used to walk to work in the dark
on the opposite side of the street
somebody always walked with him but they never met
he could only hear the boots
& when he stopped they stopped.

The new baby swayed in a canvas cot lacing his fingers
I worried in case he got curvature of the spine
Truby King said a baby needed firm support
he was a very big bright baby
the cleaner at the Queen Vic. said every morning
you mark my words that kid's been here before.

The house was bare & cold with a false gable
we had no furniture only a double mattress
on the floor a big table & two deal chairs
every morning I dressed the baby in a shrunken jacket
& caught the bus home to my mother's to nurse the child
who was dying   the house had bay windows
hidden under fir trees smothered in yellow roses
the child sat dwarfed at the end of the polished table
pale as death in the light of his four candles
singing *Little Boy Blue.*

I pushed the pram to the telephone box
I'm losing my milk I told her *I want to bring him*

home to die   Home she said   you left
home a long time ago to go with that man.

I pushed them both through the park
over the dropped leaves (his legs were crippled)
a magpie swooped down black out of the sky
& pecked his forehead   a drop of blood splashed on
his wrist   he started to cry

It took five months & everybody was angry
because the new baby was alive & cried for attention
pollen sprinkled his cheeks under the yellow roses.

When he died it was like everybody else
in the public ward with the screens around him
the big bruises spreading on his skin
his hand came up out of the sheets *don't cry*
he said *don't be sad*

I sat there overweight in my Woolworth's dress
not telling anybody in case they kept him alive
with another transfusion –

        Afterwards I sat by the gas fire
in my old dressing gown turning over the photographs
wondering why I'd drunk all that stout
& massaged my breasts every morning to be
        a good mother.

Fourth Exile's Letter

from THE MANDELSTAM LETTERS

You took away all the oceans and all the room.
You gave me my shoe-size in earth with bars around it.
Where did it get you?   Nowhere
You left me my lips, and they shape words,
    even in silence.

                                    Osip Mandelstam, Voronezh (1935)

I come home to find they have cancelled my permit
    to live in the city,
expelled from Moscow, months in the Lubianka.
It's spring, I've sold my leather-jacket
    now I wear an old coat made of dog's skin.
Along the Yaroslavl railroad the prisoners are taken
    to Siberia.

I live in Strunina in the 105 kilometre zone, we eat wild
    berries in the woods, we live like hunted animals
    in the taiga.
She spins the yarn and memorizes my verses . . .

I got into hot water in the offices of Izvestia.
They said, *Do you know what happens after you write*
    a poem like that? Three men come for you in uniform.
We live beyond the 100th kilometre, sitting out things
    in these savage times.
Moscow draws us like a magnet, stranded for one night
    in the Forbidden City we missed the last train
    back to Kalinin.
In the streets of Moscow in my dogskin jacket I am
    taken for an exile.
There is a biting wind on the bridge across the Volga,
    the wind of persecution and exile.
We trudge along to our rented room on the edge of town,
the streets are impassable with mud and snow,
    our landlady serves us tea from a samovar with
    home-made jam,
the lamps are lit before the icon, we read Pravda,

have concerts on the phonograph Dvorak
   Mussorgski   the Brandenburg Concerto,
we are part of the hare-brained upper crust, we lack
   the will to live,
let people up top meddle and murder each other,
   go to the devil   in their own sweet way,
we made a revolution   but nobody asked us to.
   Don't cry, we'll be like the saints.

We spent two months in the Writers' Rest Home in
   Samatikha, baffled by such duplicity.
There are phone calls, inquiries about our health,
   we even have ice-cream on the 1st of May!
we live in a quaint forest hut, totally isolated,
   we seem to be very big fish indeed.
They are beginning to look after us   do you think
       we have fallen into a trap?
In the morning somebody knocks quietly on the door.
Two men in uniform say *Come with us. You'll*
   have to go all the way to Siberia to mend your ways.

Everything moves so smoothly, the sleigh with the
   sheepskin rugs waiting to keep us warm,
we are treated like guests of honour, it is a very
   cold March and the pine trees crackle with frost.
The Party is an inverted church mirrored
      in the Kremlin towers.

NANCY KEESING

The Three Ring Circus Townsville!

Ring one – The three ring circus

My sharp-brained, tart-tongued mother is old and potty
At ninety-one. Her hair flies like white cloud,
(She always wore an 'invisible net'), all spotty
With milky coffee the front of her clothes no matter
How kind and careful the nurses. Her fingers fumble,
Her mouth mumbles and drops burst out in a spatter.

The nurses love her because she does not cry out
But sings them French songs I'd never heard her sing
While the other old mad creatures rant, weep, shout.

Nothing perturbs her. Not news of death nor sorrow
Within her family. She thinks we've come from New Zealand
By the old *Wanganui* and will sail back there tomorrow.

She who bought Streetons, two Turners and a Rembrandt etching
Does 'Painting' at Occupational Therapy.
Colouring-in it is; she adores it. Watching
Her thin hands holding the brush I think I will die
On the spot. Such pity I have for her. She's lived
Past what she would ever have wished. How can one cry
For an ancient baby who sings French songs for the nurses?
'She's always so full of fun,' they say. I could kill them.
They're turning my mother into a three ring circus.

Ring two – Sing no French songs for me

Miss Elspeth Kelsey, my mother's governess
Taught her most exquisite French, and singing games.
She, in her nineties, crazed and memory-less
Twists her fleshless fingers into frames
And flickering signals from her schoolroom time,
Caricaturing childhood with jingle and rhyme.

Six sous ci
Six sous ça
Six sous sont ces
Saucissons là!

Miss Kelsey instilled stiff manners and self control.
Oft-quoted Miss Kelsey was *our* despair. Forbidden
Were temper, loud voices, soup slopped round a bowl,
Uneaten crusts, et-cet-era. Overlaid, hidden
By layers of life, house, children, our eccentric father
Miss Kelsey has re-emerged, or her spectre, rather.

Mad grey creatures widdershins shriek for food.
Eat spoonsful of sugar, pinch morsels from a neighbour's plate.
My mother reproves: 'Sit up! Be quiet! Be good!
No pudding for you if you carry on this rate!'
The nurses applaud and approve. I pity her most
When she speaks with the voice of Elspeth Kelsey's ghost.

Ring three – Misunderstood, or 'shagreen' is pronounced 'chagrin'

My grandfather's old-age child and youngest daughter
Was frail and skinny and 'spoiled' her sisters said.
And now she's ninety-one and they are dead.

Before she was out of the schoolroom her sisters were married –
The great beauty, barren; the elegant mother of three.
My mother put up her hair and travelled. She tarried
Bemused by Ruskin in Florence. In gay *Paris*
My grandmother decked her ugly duckling like a swan.
My mother went overboard for Gilbert Murray
And made herself classical swathes of white chiffon.
And her old-age father said 'Charming' and didn't worry.

She smoked cigarettes in an outré shagreen holder.
Her sisters cried, 'Heavens! What will Father say?'
'It is his gift,' smirked my blue-stocking mother, grown older
Than her envious older sisters. 'Well, put it away,'
They snapped. 'You're back in Australia now, for good
And your flaunting fads will not be understood.'

Misunderstood she languished for London and Venice.
The Bulletin published her essay on the Murray translations.
My grandmother took her calling. Her nemesis
Was delicate teas and drawing-room conversations.

Grandfather grew doddery old. She, dreadfully bored.
Her sisters said: 'We told you you'd be sorry,
The way you dress and talk, men are over-awed.
Come down a peg and we'll find you a catch to marry.'

My mother laughed, blew smoke in their eyes and, teasing,
Snared the catch of the year, a hero from the war,
The artistic, eccentric puritan, Gordon Keesing,
And found she had got herself more than she bargained for
Or ever quite came to terms with: my complex father
Not to be wheedled or twisted to anyone's whim.
They dearly loved, but did not understand each other.
In her second childhood she never speaks of him.

Female spider – spider female

Legs, wicked, slender, hairy.
Her body surfaces shine.
Her own juices supply
Trap and lure and line.
Dew and early sun
Display the shapes of her cruel
Festoons in innocent trees;
She glitters, a central jewel
Or, evilly immobile
Lurking in curved leaf
Her crouch is the shape of her victims'
And of her own death.

> Defiant of gravity, she
> On slightest currents of air
> Projects herself towards
> Any direction where
> Something vulnerable,
> Something delectable thrives
> Secure in her own skills
> And spells to disfigure lives.
> She has eaten and spat out
> Her husband, her other men.
> Her hunger, insatiable
> Turns to her own children.

Kissing, caressing, licking
She feeds on brains and hearts
Hopes and accomplishments
And other delicate parts
Of those she has entrapped
In webs of fascination
Nor does she abandon victims –
Their shells, in sad damnation
Broken, living-not-living
She serves and cossets to ensure
Her reputation for love
Total, selfless and pure.

ELIZABETH JOLLEY

Neighbour Woman on the Fencing Wire

So you've bought this place well let me tell you
straight away your soil's no good all salt even a
hundred and sixty feet down and up on the slopes
is outcrops of granite and dead stumps of dead
wood nothing'll grow there we know we've tried
what the crows don't take the rabbits and bandicoots
will have your creek floods in winter and
in summer it's dried the water's all salt there
too your sheep'll either starve or drown and if a
calf gets born it'll not be able to get up that's
the kind of place this is and what's more you've
poison weed all over your block so if you
put stock you'll lose the lot and another thing
there was a snake on our place last year and it shot
through into yours and I daresay it's still there and
where there's one snake there's sure to be another
and there's been some terrible accidents round here
only last week a man just married a week
thought he'd fix his roof and fell through the rafters
and his wife only a young thing found him hanging
dead and then there was that pig ate a woman's
baby right in front of her door mind you I always say –

JILL HELLYER

Jonah's Wife

A likely story, she said.
You fled to Tarshish from
the presence of the Lord
and now you're telling us
you were cast overboard.
A likely story, she said,
climbing cold into her cold bed.

In the belly of a whale!
You, old man, who fear
the Lord's wrath and mine
coming home like this
and spinning such a yarn.
The belly of a whale!
A quaint excuse . . . I know a likelier tale.

A touching story, she said,
to say they cast you out
for being troublesome . . .
and well they might! Your own
wife knows what shores you've swum.
But swallowed by a whale! she said
laughing cold into her cold bed.

GRACE PERRY

Waiting for the birth

1

She is alone now

steers haunch off head down
the old dog does not bark
head on knee he licks my hand

blue banners wave gold words

today is the cold handkerchief
across a face
a child's nose bleeding

in the sea of oats
she is a monument
legs spread   face calm

the deep wells
withhold the burden of world
                              blood
                              water

pause between gesture and gesture
life   death
            postponed

2

Sky is a bronze plate
            balanced
            on scribble gums

she makes a nest
threading thistles
for a thorny bed
other animals back away
            watch beyond the shade

I sit still

we murmur to one another

the bulge   the bag
birthwater
white front feet
white face
          slide towards me
the body
speckled fish
drowsy lizard

she moans and lifts her head
to lick the seacaul
from the bluetongued mouth

she does not hurry
examining the limp shape
grunts   goes on licking
over and over

fishskin dries red curls
    ears move   eyes open

he is alive

FAY ZWICKY

Ark Voices

MRS NOAH SPEAKS

Lord, the cleaning's nothing.
What's a pen or two?
Even if the tapir's urine
Takes the paint clean off
There's nothing easier.

But sir, the care!

I used to dream perpetually
About a boat I had to push
(yes, push) through a stony town
without water
There was no river and no sea and yet
I pushed a boat against a tide.
It wouldn't float although I pulled and
hauled, my flesh eddying,
drifting with the strain of it.
Is this a dream?
Fibre my blood, sir.

The speckled pigeon and the tawny owl
swoop by
                They coax me to the edge.

To save to save merely – no matter
what or whom – to save.

Sweep and push of waves against the sides.
Our raft is delicate and our fire
turns wood to ashes.

He takes it well
and Shem and Ham *do* help – you can't expect
too much of anyone can you and
Japhet's still a kid. Their wives are
young and tremble in the rain
their wits astray.

As soon as we're born
we're all astray – at least
You seem to think it's so or else
why this?

I know you promised us a landing but
what a price!
We're dashed from side to side
we strike through spray
the foam blinds Noah till he
cannot steer.
Even the mightiest creature cowers in his
stall panting, snorting in the welter,
bursting prayers upon your path
of righteousness.

Comfort enough I'm not.
To feed and clothe, to bind a scratch I can.

We once moved quiet in our lives
Looked steadily ahead. When I was small
there were no roads across the mountains
no boats or bridges over water.
We farmed, lived simple, circumscribed.
Our birds and beasts delivered their young
in peace.
            The trees grew tall and now and
then I pocketed a speckled egg, could climb
and peer into the nests of starlings.
Height and blossom.

Then we lived neighbourly with our birds.
Creation, your handiwork, was one.
No good and bad – just men and women.
But with your sages came the rub. We tripped
over our charity. Duty-fettered, love
tumbled like a lightning-stricken tower.

Noah is incorruptible and good, a large
sweet soul.
Sir, I have tried to be!
But does the frog whose home was in a well
assail an ocean?

How does the summer gnat approach the ice?
The flood in which you throne us is to the
universe a puddle in a marsh. Of all the myriad
creatures you have made, man is but one, the
merest tip of hair upon a stallion's rump.

Noah looks into space.
He sees the small as small
The great as great.
He sees, goes fearless at the sight.
I see the small as too little
the great as too much.
Does this diminish me?

He looks back to the past
grieves not over what is distant.
I mourn the wrack, the rock under the
blue sea, our old wound, the
dismantling storm and cannot
thank you. Helpless with what I am
what can I do? This pitted flesh and
madness in my heart, rage at my fear
of you. Am I thus harmless?
Strangers in this ark, this one small 'Yes'
afloat on a vast 'No', your watery negative.

Noah stares impassive through the foam.
I trust in him although our woe, the
trap of my young body, cracked his trust
in me. I bend but do not break under your
chilling stars.

Even the wolves, the tigers must be fed
in these deep-laden waters. Else we are
all drowned bones. Intercede with him
for me, speechless and unspoken to, the
comic keeper of his house.
My sons are fraught with wives, have
waded into deep waters.
A full ship and homeward bound – Yes,
I'm just about to lance the horse's leg.

A large sweet soul and incorruptible
I said. Or have I seen the great as
too much yet again? The speckled pigeon
and the tawny owl have drawn me to the edge.
The drowned folk call to me:
Deliver us from harm!

Deliver, sir, deliver them
and all of us . . .

The Poet Puts It Away

Keeping his beard on, he moved
into hand-stitched shoes
7-league suits: the buckle's
wink was dim.

                Losing altitude he
entered the 'diviner heaven of prose':
getting closer to himself.
Out of gear
and often in the wrong key,
had haemorrhoids, was ethically in a
mess and, for the umpteenth time, his
daemonic was slipping.

Scholarly research can
excavate the problem from St Paul
till 1980: called psychohistory,
some things are better left alone.

                More subjectively
and not sober, he indicated equally
Dr Heinrich Hoffman (circa 1840) and
his mother (definitely 1907 although
she preferred 1915) for cutting him off
in all directions:

'The door flew open, in he ran,
The great, long, red-legg'd scissorman
Oh! children see! the tailor's come
And caught out little Suck-a-Thumb'

A close shave either way.

Ever alert for women booze and chocolate
he committed 354 fornications (at least
half were under-age) off his own bat
though he called it 'getting laid':

'Mama had scarcely turn'd her back,
The thumb was in, Alack! Alack!'

               Countless airy lies
laid out like glowing rugs for his
imaginative inspection; constant coveting
of his neighbour's ass (he moved house
often); the theft of three books:

the Gideon Bible from the
Port Hedland Motor Hotel
(the word of God ought to
be free and the Gideons
whoever they are want you
to steal it so they can put
another in its place for
another lying Priapus to
simmer down with after
multiple campus fucks);
Aristotle's *Nichomachean Ethics*
(which he assumed nobody would
ever read and he never got
around to it either); and
Henry Miller's *Cosmological Eye*
(which ought to have proved
orgasmic but turned out to be
vaguely mystic and
put him to sleep. Quickly).

Two cats and a dog met their end by
his motor vehicle, a thousand
winged insects by his hand:

   'Here is cruel Frederick, see!
   A horrid wicked boy was he'

His father was anything but honoured
his mother positively dishonoured,
hacked up, hidden and easily discovered:

   'Let me see if Frederick can
   Be a little gentleman'

Took God's name in vain daily
put himself inexorably into every
poem without even a decorous
pretence of self-distrust for which
he received high praise.

      Slandered the
Sicilian next door, put away
5000 litres of whisky in
10 years, made his wives
altars of stone and
sacrificed them to
punk rock:

and no (with a sideways look)
today he wasn't friendly either.

Erect in the middle of
thunderings and lightnings
he struck:
      more poems in him
than he'd hoped for but
more than he wished.

      They
had a way of telling
the truth and believing
himself alone in the
storm he heard
none of it.

JENNIFER STRAUSS

Guenevere Dying

And when Queen Guenevere understood that King Arthur was dead and all the
noble knights, Sir Mordred and all the remnant, then she stole away with five ladies
with her, and so she went to Amesbury. And there she let make herself a nun, and
wore white clothes and black, and (as) great penance she took upon her as ever
did sinful woman in this land. And never creature could make her merry, but ever
she lived in fasting, prayers and almsdeeds, that all manner of people marvelled
how virtuously she was changed.

Sir Thomas Malory

In the cell for the dying you can see the sky,
'Not,' said the priest 'to pleasure the rotting flesh
But to nourish the labouring soul
With Heaven's symbol.' I watch the snow,
The first of winter, soft and insubstantial,
Goose feathers drifting curled in the quiet air.
In Cornwall, storms will be whipping the black waves
As the white gulls twist in the hurling gale,
Screeching defiant against the battering cliffs.
There is a death for you: but not for me –
I owe the abbess a good death, a soft settling,
As that snowflake clings at the window
Petal, pear-bloom . . .

The pear-tree was a parting gift from Cador;
'A Cornish tree for a Cornish bird,' he said,
Putting a good face on it once the oaths were sworn.
'Gwen, Gwen,' he had cried 'should I let you fly
Into the sweet cage, be lured from your wildness?'
But I could not hear for the dancing of blood
In my ears, in my toes, in my finger-tips,
As Arthur was deaf to politic Merlin
'She is not good, my Lord, for you to have.'

How we hated each other, Merlin and I.
'Men do not love,' I mocked 'to be robbed of their boys,
But a grown man should be free of tutors, surely.'

I came between them. He was right,
I was not good for Arthur. No-one asks
Was Arthur good for me. At Winchester
The moment the crown touched, Gwen died in his eyes.
It was a queen he saw: his queen, his heir.
Well, God knows I was willing – how I wept
Monthly a tear for every drop of blood,
And the petals fell but no fruit followed.

Three Springs I lay in the orchard grass,
Watching its white flowers dapple
The shining sun. In Autumn as we rode,
Arthur and I, to hunt by the river,
He checked there, frowning. 'A pretty thing,
But barren: let the gardeners
Burn it. We owe the land
Good husbandry!' Next Spring I saw the sun
Naked over Lancelot's shoulder.

'Consider' says the priest 'God's mercy,
Which makes of you
A brand plucked from the burning.'
                    I thought of Lancelot
Riding over the green field to save me from the stake.
Trumpets blowing, brassy in the sun,
Pennants in wind, the red blood spilling.
Men slaughter men with sword and lance
'Honourably': trees and women they burn –
Always afraid of female blood.
Barren, barren . . .
                    Burning, burning . . .

If he had let things be, I would not now
Owe to the abbess a good death, who took me in
While sisters clutched their uncontaminated skirts
As if I carried lust's infection with me.
A jest. Honest desire had long withered in me,
Starved in that garden of cultivated souls.
Arthur 'must' burn me: Lancelot 'must' save me –
How I dangled meanings for others to snatch
And set like stones in moral gold.

I am bruised all over on men's imperatives.
Lancelot 'must be freed'. I watched his feet
Dragging to make an honest woman of me.
He might have freed himself with one honest word
When first he wished to go: but I must stage
Pageants of renunciation for him, put ashes in my hair
For penitence, be prisoner to his codes –
Oh noble cages, strange and golden:
Crown, Honour, Chivalry. Ashes from my pear-tree
Blew through the casement onto my marriage bed.
It is time they buried me,
I have been long dying.

MARGARET SCOTT

Grandchild

Early this morning, when workmen were switching on lights
in chilly kitchens, packing their lunch-boxes
into their Gladstone bags, starting their utes in the cold
and driving down quiet streets under misty lamps,
my daughter bore a son. Nurses sponged him clean
as the glittering shingle of suburbs beside the river
waned to a scattered glimmer of pale cubes.
We met at half-past twelve in a ward crowded
with people busy with parcels and extra chairs.
A bunch of flowers fell on the floor. We passed
the baby round. His dark head lay in my hand
like a fruit. He seemed to be dwelling on something
half-remembered, puckering his brow, occasionally
flexing fingers thin and soft as snippets of mauve string.
Far below in the street lunch-time crowds flowed out
among the traffic. Girls went arm in arm on high
heels. An ambulance nosed into a ground-floor bay.
A clerk strode in the wind with a streaming tie.
Beyond the office blocks and the estuary, in Santa Fé,
Northampton or the other side of town, a young man
may be gripping a girl's hand as they climb upstairs.
She is wearing a cotton dress. Her sandals slip
on metal treads. She laughs, embarrassed, excited
at being desired so urgently in the
minutes before this grandchild's wife is conceived.
And his best friend, whose parents quarrel all day
about leaving Greece, is lying perhaps in his cot
on a balcony, watching his fat pink hands and woolly sleeves
swatting at puffs of cloud in the airy blue.
News he may break to our boy in some passage-way
in a house we've never seen is breeding now
in the minds of pensive children queuing by Red Cross
trucks, or curled like foetuses deep under warm quilts
as the long ship-wrecking roar of the distant sea
slides to the coming of night and fades away.

The Black Swans

for Ruth Blair

The children have taken the boat round the point today.
I sit on the sand with the new binoculars
trying to match the coast of this island bay
with my exile's map. Close by, a white-faced heron
waits for fish. Each hunched in a separate need
we watch the three black swans come out to feed.
The black swans! In Jonson's day the wits
made comic mirrors called 'Antipodes',
mocking the times with virtuous whores, white crows,
ascetic drunks, and black swans, nesting in walking trees.
Even now these birds surprise. Emblems of
paradox, they ride in their dipping line on the blue sea,
sombre as slow, archaic, high-prowed
funeral ships, with the plain absurdity
of cut-out toys, a scrap of nursery frieze.
But when I turn the glasses on a wing, a tough
red beak, a savage scarlet eye, they're suddenly rough
and real, and all themselves.
Their feathers are dull with salt, tattered by wind
to makeshift heaps of burnt-out odds and ends –
a ruffle of charred paper, a draggled quill,
a stirring of buried lice. A neck bends,
thick as a child's arm, to a pointed, violent head,
red eye intent with the beat of scaly leg,
with the thrust of working webs in the clear wave.
They pass like the last of a tribe too wild to beg,
like run-down pirates, gipsies, renegades
with broken teeth, bandanas, belts of knives.
And so they go each morning of their lives
to where the pickings are – as ape men went
or my father in his suit, as the fishing crane
goes out and the fisherman.
When evening comes they travel back again
and sleep as everyone sleeps – and has slept – who must be fed,
whatever coast he maps, whatever stars
shine through the lappings of myth on his quiet bed.

ANTIGONE KEFALA

Freedom Fighter

A freedom fighter, she said
lighting the gas stove.
In the mountains we fought
great days . . .
the words stubborn
weary in the shabby kitchen
with the yellowed fridge
and the tinted photograph
of the dead husband.
The house full of morose
rooms suffocated with rugs.

We came out on the low verandah
her heavy stockings pitch black
the rough spun dress the
indigo blue of some wild flower
the Sunday neighbourhood still asleep.
Come again, she said indifferently
watching the windy street
and the Town Hall squatting
on its elephant legs,
come again.

KATHERINE GALLAGHER

Passengers to the City

This morning she is travelling
eyes steeled on her knitting,
while the man next to her
from time to time turns his head,
glances briefly at the fiery wool
then looks away.

He is silent as a guard, and she
never speaks. Are they together, some pair
perfectly joined by silence?
Or are they today's complete strangers?

I'll never know, left simply
to knit them together – characters in a story,
a middle-aged couple on a train
waiting for love's fable to happen
to them, for their old lives to be
swept aside, changed, changed –
as she keeps knitting, bumping him
occasionally, at which he shrugs,
turns his head quickly
not like a lover, but content.

Concerning the Fauna

When I see kangaroos on the screen,
I take in the landscape
at one miraculous jump.

It's the same with koalas –
my stomach lifts,
I start climbing the nearest tree.

I'm an old hand now.

Once I saw a famous politician
fill a meeting-hall:
his subject, 'Kangaroos and koalas –
our national identity.'

People listened rapt:
by the end of the evening
we were all either
jumping or climbing.

Finally in the hullaballoo
the police were called –
only the fastest got away.

JUDITH RODRIGUEZ

How do you know it's the right one?

Can you play it on a keyboard?
On one string?
Is it partial to silence?

Can you exalt it
continuously?
Can you debase it?

Can you look at it curdled
and pasty
in the glass after midnight?

And eat it and drink it
whatever –
it with its memories

and malaise, years and days of it?
Must you have it?
Will you love it or live with it?

The letter from America

The letter from America
drops in the box.
The family is impressed.
The postie walks on
uplifted by the revelatory postmark
and stamps from America.

Someone in the house
stands unlit watching
for just these wings
and a personal print-out
of the latest state of affections
and rates of exchange.

The letter is orbiting stars
here and America.
Our sightings are less frequent.
When it nears
conditions are unstable,
the static abhorrent

the letter from America
has made an incision
along the threshold.
It applies reassuring
suggestions and alternative promises.
It encloses a contract.

No-one will violate
its supersensitive triangle.
Suddenly it exploded!
It was so white:
The letter from America has vanished
leaving a zip-code –

someone in the house
is counting the promises,
is hoarding the answer.
Someone in the window
is watching the windy day,
is mourning, is mourning.

Eskimo occasion

I am in my Eskimo-hunting-song mood,
Aha!
The lawn is tundra   the car will not start
the sunlight is an avalanche   we are avalanche-struck at our breakfast
struck with sunlight through glass   me and my spoonfed daughters
out of this world in our kitchen.

I will sing the song of my daughter-hunting,
Oho!
The waves lay down   the ice grew strong
I sang the song   of dark water under ice
the song of winter fishing   the magic for seal rising
among the ancestor masks.

  - waited by water to dream new spirits,
Hoo!
The water spoke   the ice shouted
the sea opened   the sun made young shadows
they breathed my breathing   I took them from deep water
I brought them fur-warmed home.

I am dancing the years of the two great hunts,
Ya-hay!
It was I who waited   cold in the wind-break
I stamp like the bear   I call like the wind of the thaw
I leap like the sea spring-running.   My sunstruck daughters splutter
and chuckle and bang their spoons:

Mummy is singing at breakfast and dancing!
So big!

The mudcrab-eaters

Nothing lovers in their forties do together
        that they don't, you'd say, repeat.
        But then, this day, what others here
        so feast, rising on the lean threat
        of the night apart? or so taste
        and toast their exquisite lot?

        Who else at Gambaro's is happy?
        With dolphin glances serving
        each other, the lovers sit, sea-delight
        lightening air. And though
they night and morning years-long sat down to mudcrab,
        they have never eaten mudcrab before.

black and white, mostly white:
a style of living

How strangely strut
on days of mild lifting air
our white refusals: watts
rammed down an eye's well;
scorings of a traffic-glove index
chastening abandoned ways
kerbed henceforth to bear
only blanched bridals
processionally ambulant . . .

how amazedly haunt
glades of the soul, rumours
of pallid night, and day
swarthy, our colours awry
in frenzies of late neon
and noon's sealed cell.
Agreed rituals shawl
shadow about our houses,
coil light inside.

Houses are not for hiding.
Air coloured clear
passing through intimates
wide green, lofty blue.
But trellis and blind remain
to propose that screened and slit
and safe, we occupy
plastered pigeon-holes, white-
ceilinged, white-silled, unremitting –

you'd need to be limed to the soul
to be there without notice:
neat as eggs, null as ever and ever.
Hiding, for flesh and blood
and mind, means finding
flesh and blood and mind
blood-coloured, to bleed on. Vines
tower above whitewash-shovers.
This poem is not about houses.

Bivalve

Conforming right now to the norms
neither of courtship nor teaching
the open side of my face spreads out
the closed side tightens.

If this goes on
my head will be a clam slewed sideways
in all the stew of my sea-bed spaces
and will never sit straight on
such the push and wash of its element.

If you try to get round it
you will only be taken in
by the bland loom of liquid expansions.
On the other tack
there's no open approach to the simple
hinge built round with rock
precisely

and I do not despise it;

the wide side of me there with its undulant plush
expanding exploring incessantly
and its nerve-ends softer than water
shrieking on grit and ululating at ease
is there to supply the fit
of my unprised grip
my quick and holding bit.

One side the drying knot.
The other
the pulsing mass shimmers
to farm its parasite
and silkenly tugs my focal creature tight
in its grotto of blood
usages of light.

Towards Fog

The quality of fog is that it has style but no detail.
Though detected in a state of nuance, it cannot be caught at it.
I try with a 2B – softly – with a 6 or 8B – I am gradual as growing –
still there are lines, parts, separations. Fog has none.
When was a photograph of fog, a film of fog moving,
ever so diffuse, directionless, and all-round-clammy?
And the incuriosity of fog is beyond everything.

There are times I want to go back to somewhere like beginning.
The concept of a cell is too advanced for what I want to be, sometimes.
Words are cellular, and baulk at it: fog is not-saying.
Fog engulfs. Devours, with no process. Fog is instead of.
Fog extends. Fog bulks. It is nothing you ever see in profile, yet there .

What is *there*? I put out my hand. Is that a handful of fog?

Does it flow through? And can I expel it with a willed clenching?
Or invite it with nebulous fingers, tendons in concert –
    the hand half-opening

Mind revving up to understand, body boggling
at the falling to inorganic, the going nerveless;
both fall short, bailed up on recognized borders.
The true photograph of fog would disappear,
its corners sucked into monochrome lack of point.
And the drawing of fog would be made with
horizonless sky and land for a pencil.
And the poem of fog would fold
round the wire-thin word *today-as-usual*
all the sounds, ideas of all kinds of being
in a more than pastoral silence.

The man as fog does not bear thinking of
Green though the slopes are, after.

I displace fog, yet it is inward with me.
I can't do fog. Never, perhaps, to be done with it –
exhalations from a deep place, earth-rumours
fragile and huge, a beauty of a threat
there's no dealing with.

SYLVIA KANTARIS

The Tenth Muse

My muse is not one of the nine nubile
daughters of Mnemosyne
in diaphanous nightshifts
with names that linger in the air
like scent of jasmine or magnolia
on Mediterranean nights.
Nor was any supple son of Zeus appointed
to pollinate my ear with poppy dust
or whispers of sea-spray.
My muse lands with a thud
like a sack of potatoes.
He has no aura.
The things he grunts are things
I'd rather not hear.
His attitude is 'Take it or leave it, that's
the way it is', drumming his fingers
on an empty pan by way of music.
If I were a man I would enjoy
such grace and favour,
tuning my fork to Terpsichore's lyre,
instead of having to cope with this dense
late-invented eunuch
with no more pedigree than the Incredible Hulk,
who can't play a note
and keeps repeating 'Women
haven't got the knack'
in my most delicately strung and scented ear.

Package for the Distant Future

Dear Inheritor,
Since you have dared to open this container
you must be living in some far-distant,
unimaginable future,
and I am writing from a time of earth
before your world began –
we call it the era of Modern Man
(a bit after the Cro-Magnon).
Enclosed you will find evidence
of our existence:
a skein of yellow silk;
a carving of a child of unknown origin
with normal limbs and features;
a violin;
some lilac seeds;
the Song of Solomon.
The selection is not scientific, just
flotsam and jetsam of our civilisation.
I hope you like them.
We had a lot of things we did not like
and could have lived without.
Do not invent gods.
I hope the earth is nearly clean again.
Sow the lilac seeds in damp soil
and if they grow and flower, and if you can,
smell them after rain.

from News From the Front*

XXII

Just as I was swallowing my valium
he ran his little finger down my spine
and made me choke. He wanted me to stare
into a looking-glass like that fat Venus
by Velazquez – to make me calm, he said:
'Women should be calm as the moon no matter
what storms break around her'. And certainly
the moon was there in painting after painting,
pale and anaemic like a reflection
from a ten-watt lamp. In that light it isn't
possible to see things as men see them,
but at the Picasso exhibition
next morning, we saw woman after woman
with sickle moons instead of heads, all mouth,
stuck with spikes along the cutting-edge:
Mary Magdalen about to savage Christ;
Charlotte Corday tearing into a phallus . . .
If that's the way they all really see us,
no wonder they shut us up in mirrors.

XXIV

'Sóror Vidante do Céu, Florbela Espanca,
Teresa of Avila . . .' She stopped. 'Ave Maria!'
I said, and laughed, but she didn't get the joke.
She lay there telling her fingers like a rosary
and stuck at three obscure names – all nuns,
moved to minor verse by their religion.
'Nuns have a slight advantage over ordinary women',
I said, 'because they can devote themselves
to higher things. They're more like men whereas
a normal woman's function is to be a mistress,
wife and mother, and work at being as attractive
as she can. It's an important occupation. The world

would be in a fine mess without such feminine
devotion to our basic needs, and even our more
elevated undertakings. Think of Shakespeare,
Petrarch, Donne – just to mention three poets
everybody's heard of – they all used women
for inspiration (and if it hadn't been for Dante
Beatrice would have remained a mere nobody).'
And then I put my hand out tenderly to pat
her head, but the Bolshie cow suddenly shot
out of bed and hauled her jeans and boots on.
I wonder what Dante would have done in my place
if Beatrice had stood over him like that wearing
all that gear and spat in his face.

* 'News From the Front' was written with D.M. Thomas. They wrote alternating
poems. These two are by S.K. *eds.*

Travelogue

I don't know why it is that lean, lanky
Travelogues of poems with careful detail –
Not too much but just enough to pin
The whole length of the Nile down say –
Generally bore me stiff. It's not as if

I hadn't travelled round the world myself,
By bike, and roughed it in Baluchistan
And rounded capes and horns galore,
Attending to my light meter, and eaten
Whale flesh, raw, and dyed my teeth with betel.

It's not as if I hadn't seen the Taj Mahal
Or stood in awe at Trollfjord or looked
Into a tiger's eye in Kenya and escaped
To tell the tale I never wrote because
It makes me want to yawn. Instead I note

The things that are especially important
Like fading curtains or the way the sun
Illuminates the dust on shelves and chairs
Or picks the silver threads out from the golden
And settles squarely on my pickling jars.

Annunciation

It seems I must have been more fertile than most
to have taken that wind-blown
thistledown softly-spoken word
into my body and grown big-bellied with it.
Nor was I the first: there had been
rumours of such goings-on before my turn
came – tales of swansdown. Mine
had no wings or feathers actually
but it was hopeless trying to convince them.
They like to think it was a mystical
encounter, although they must know
I am not of that fibre – and to say I was
'troubled' is laughable.
What I do remember is a great rejoicing,
my body's arch and flow, the awe,
and the ringing and singing in my ears –
and then the world stopped for a little while.
But still they will keep on about the Word,
which is their name for it, even though I've
told them that is definitely
not how I would put it.
I should have known they'd try to take
possession of my ecstasy and
swaddle it in their portentous terminology.
I should have kept it hidden in the dark
web of my veins . . .
Though this child grows in me –
not unwanted certainly, but
not intended on my part; the risk
did not concern me at the time, naturally.
I must be simple to have told them anything.
Just because I stressed the miracle of it
they've rumoured it about the place that I'm
immaculate – but then they always were afraid
of female sexuality.
I've pondered these things lately in my mind.
If they should canonize me
(setting me up as chaste and meek and mild)
God only knows what nonsense
they'll visit on the child.

JEAN TALBOT

Muse

Planning to leave again, were you? –
pinchpenny, ponce, pack-rat!
I caught you draggle-tailed
slinking the easy way out,
hoping for disguise
in those shapeless rags!
And what's in your bag,
rag-tag, slag?
You shrug and unzip . . .

                albigensian, borsch, tantivy
                tantalize, liquorice, Lusitania . . .

    Trash, all of it!
    Take it! Good riddance!
    I've had enough!

You
look past your straggled hair
into me
and say
not one word;

but now I
am walking down the garden
past the orange-blossoms
and through the gate
with my rags, and draggled hair
and my bag of nothing.

J. S. HARRY

the gulf of bothnia

in the gulf of bothnia near the top the
salinity's between
four to six parts   per thousand
flounder & pike   live
in the same 'sea'
also seaweed & freshwater plants sit
side by side
as grandmother & grandfather
on the veranda
in their rockers   might have done
could they've lived
in the gulf of bothnia
near the top
the land is rising at one hundred millimetres
per metre per hundred years – out of the sea –
boat houses sit in cow paddocks
falling green on their knees into grass
waiting for the sea to come back
& the boats to visit –
much as grandfather & grandmother
might've waited   for 'life' to come back
to visit them
on the old-age farm – had they lived
by the gulf of bothnia near the top –
& reindeer step down the bogs
delicately
lowering   one after the other
soft
reindeer's mouths
into the rich bog plants

cows drink the sea   in the gulf of bothnia
                              near the top
fresher   water on the surface
salt-er   lower down

we are unable   to breathe
in the gulf of bothnia

though have often dreamed

of visiting   our imaginary relatives
the seaweeds & the freshwater plants

beside those ancient farms

subjective around lismore

beside a hill
growing a dense,
naturally-irregular

gumscrubhaircut

the hill growing bananas

is like a head
with a short
back-&-sides; neckhigh lumps

which could be boils or carbuncles
,on a person,
ripen aggressive, under blue,
plastic-bags –

                        aggro. packaged –
punch – like, does anyone?,
the local toughs: viceblue
but different – if a blood-eye
was *all* yous got . . .

                        & truth: we didn't
get dropped down a mineshaft
out emmaville way, as rumour puts
some locals lost; there was
a reason, for that, which drinkers
will tell you, 4 or 5
times an hour, about –

                        if you're not

local cops – though who
is growing marihuana & where
is something about which to nobody
anybody will talk – the population
of lismore
is composed
of 60,000 knees – some hairy, some balding –
that are used
to bending
to a warmer weather
as are also

the other parts   (some (4) to the going price
                          from brisbane for a contract-kill)

we left our thug the ego-poem there
bashing up the local toughs

though outclassed by a deeper light
mafiablue   coming through
from the other side of his glass

& just pissed off

fire flaring at night through fields of burning sugar
& anger   red on black   complete the lismore 'i'

uncle with currawongs

whisky fug
in a rainy kitchen
uncle with cracked
rib & concussion
drinking
a bottle a day
spider spinning
in the downstairs
lavatory
legs waving
weaving 8
hours a day
ants crawling in
out of their
rain soused
earthholes
uncle writing
weaves of
remembered oral history –
wilder & wilder –
in mince-coloured texta –
his account of
his grandfather's
handed down
family legends
of campbell ades jamison
& robinson –
larger & larger –
jamison who got his
sir-hood from
the king of
sweden for
curing the swedish
navy of scurvy
back in the days of
napoleon's wars –
a campbell whose

on-credit gold dredge
fell   into a river
under the mine
to bankrupt him
with the champagne
at the first gold bucket
raised
still fresh bubbles in his mouth
& in the mouths of those who
drank with him
to the gold
at whatever   then
pub was nearest to
the old
lambing flats' gold mines –
outside the old –
gold black-centred
press-stud eyes
of the 8 or 10
senior currawongs
peering from their rain
soused branch
into the whisky-fugged
stove-fumed kitchen
windows shut
for the drought-breaking
easter '83 rain –
currawongs peering anxiously
at uncle's violent arm moves
& jumping – at the
unnatural thunder
of voice & table-bangs –
as he wrote
gesticulated &
sometimes remembered –
back from the bloody
century of the bushrangers
dr. campbell & ben hall –
(hall mad with bullet-pain –

wanting to shoot
the doc & take his horse –
once the bullet was out –
being   talked out of it –
no other doc
for 200 miles –
& the doctor had
no other horse –
to cover the beat –
if hall-gang
got shot up again)
the wild wary black birds
waiting
for quiet
to fall on their dinner branch
so they could get on
with the serious business
of grabbing the meat

the poem films itself

Down the slimy rope   into the impossible!
The insides heave   somehow they got the camera down inside
                    the alimentary tract
The poem as a historical drama or epic
by shakespeare or a drunken lamington by somebody french whose
    names
our memories'd glided over (elision   marked by ampersand:
    digestion omitted)
will be filmed in prose our new technique (perfect
    for moribund structuralism)   The costumes
will appear to be modern, say crudely

*early*modern   ashbery or o'hara (we will not know either of
    them well enough   to differentiate)
with a few loops of pointlessly-picked-over intestine   (It would
    be 'hard'
to establish   a particular crow was here)
Though our techniques are the shirts we are betting
our horses' lives on, their bloodlines (techniques', shirts', horses')
    like those of the   abused, & fictive, 'crow',
'derive'   from the ancients & cannot be said to be authentically
'ours'   yet still the pace carries us, into the
future with a marvellous momentum We are like

the élan about to drive a gothic cathedral
upward   into havens of print/sky-high!/   happy?   heavenly?
    (exit arsehole as might be
expected)   the mixed
naturalism, & the absurd, trade-marking   the content local,
    a few flashes of unparrotlike
environmental realism, yet to be added, for the risk . . .

Notwithstanding
                    dead animals rising on our tongues (soap, soup,
the leather we've been chewing, round the holes
                    in our spirits' feet where the thaw, as a
melting joke leaves gangrene green as agony)
what sincerely gets to us is   : a kind of food-poisoning

: that we are   still here   as if saving cents for a 3rd row seat
                     where
we don't want to sit   & are   already . . . too close up . . .
     from a
3rd row seat, the soundtrack-roar
                     's quite deafening . . .
                     (& peering)   : the screen immense in front of us
(Mute Nausea   saving up   to pay
to be itself & dead?) while from the backrow stalls we do
                     not have the bread for, they say   you can almost
see, & hear, from there . . .
it could be little boy blue or hamlet   who was the one . . .
                     by the needs of the drama managed . . .
to get   the shiv dug in   himself: right
                     place &
job well-done . . . the real, irrelevant bagpipes wailing
                     frail but true, outside, (us liking them – but better:)
next role will play us into death

ROSEMARY NISSEN

The Day We Lost the Volkswagen

During a momentary lull in her head,
the poor old thing lost her grip.
The boat she was towing towed her instead
ponderously down the slip,
backwards into the water.

For a swirling moment she almost floated,
she thought of setting sail.
But her bum tilted, her britches bloated –
she was heavy in the tail –
and the sly seaweed caught her.

I thought even then she might make a try
(she seemed to be righting her flank)
but she spun gravely, one eye on the sky,
gave a dignified splutter and sank.
The sea frothed briefly.

I don't know – she wasn't the kind to drift,
much less come apart at the seams.
But the sails and the clouds that day had a lift,
and perhaps she had some dreams.
It was a damn nuisance, chiefly.

O

O is blonde
a pale egg
the shape of arms and legs around you
it is what we say
when we hear of death
or love
but we say it silently of love
because then it is the shape of a bullet
it is too oval to utter

it is a bubble when we must make a sound
but do not really wish to
yes it is fragile
but it is also strong as a stone
the sound a woman makes
when she remembers centuries of men
or a particular man
it can be sung up and down the scale
with love

it is the shape of the cave's entrance
and of the rock at the tomb
the trail of the earth round the sun
spinning O around O
it is perfect
it is the sound made when the arrow strikes
it's the bullseye
the death rattle
and while we are living
the sound and shape of love

The Kites

Here are two people
walking into a room
I am inside one of them
suddenly they teeter
as if afraid
and fall on each other
like broken kites
they flap and buck
zigzagging across the floor

one turns for a moment
her naked back
the pale wooden bone
of the kite
she cannot see this
because I am inside her

over and over round and round
she tugs at the string
in his hand

her hand is on his face
as they flap and strain
until falling
in a mass of silk and broken wood
it's a sight
it would hurt to watch
something so lovely
in one great gust
it is over
the air has gone

Breasts

As I lean over to write
one breast warm as a breast from the sun
hangs over as if to read what I'm writing
these breasts always want to know everything
sometimes exploring the inside curve of my elbow
sometimes measuring a man's hand
lying still as a pond
until he cannot feel he is holding anything
but water
then he dreams he is floating

in the morning my breast is refreshed
and wants to know something new
although it is soft it is also ambitious
we never speak
but I know my breast knows me more than I do
prying hanging over fences
observant as a neighbour
or eager as a woman wanting to gossip
they tell me nothing
but they say quite a lot about me

there is a dark blue river vein here
straggling down taking its time
to the little pale strawberry
picked too soon and left too long
in the punnet in a warm shop

when I lie
these breasts spread like spilt milk
and standing naked in the sea
float like figs
as you will realise
these are my body's curious fruit
wanting to know everything
always getting there first
strange as white beetroot
exotic as unicorns

useless as an out of order dishwasher
more of a nuisance than anything else

some men seem to think highly of them
peering and staring
what they don't know is the breast stares straight back
interested as a reporter

some love them
and invest them with glamour
but like life they are not glamourous
merely dangerous

Eve

Let's face it
Eden was a bore
nothing to do
but walk naked in the sun
make love
and talk
but no one had any problems
to speak of
nothing to read
a swim
or lunch might seem special
even afternoon tea wasn't invented
nor wine

a nap might be a highlight
no radio
perhaps they sang a bit
but as yet no one had made up
many songs

and after the honey moon
wouldn't they be bored
walking and talking

with never a worry in the world
they didn't need to invent an atom
or prove the existence of God

no it had to end
Eve showed she was the bright one
bored witless by Adam
no work
and eternal bliss
she saw her chance
they say the snake tempted her to it
don't believe it
she bit because she hungered
to know
the clever thing
she wasn't kicked out
she walked out

JAN OWEN

Swimming Instructor

(for Mona Lisa in the fifth lane)

Lips straight from the Quattrocento, at each end
a secret curlicue on a face as poised and round
as the smiling angel of Rheims surveying the world of men.
and a neck pure Primavera. Her green T-shirt's skin-tight
on breasts so high and full they're made to clasp.
Around her, four small boys of seven or eight
bob like apples in a barrel, shriek and splutter and gasp.
The echoes and reflections bounce off water and wall,
cross-currents of noise, drunken ripples of light.
She moves as evenly as a tide backwards along the lane
a small head pressed against her belly; backstrokes
faltering left and right, she guides each one in turn:
'Point your toes Michael . . . Head back, Luke,' she calls above the din.
Small knobs hard with cold, they flail and flounder on.
It's Sunday morning, the fathers have brought them down.
Men nearing forty now, they wait in the humid air,
fidget on benches at the side
and stare at their boisterous offspring and at her.
Their thoughts lap round like water, aching to touch,
as each little boy splashes towards horizons
green as promises, ripe as pippins in May.
The lesson done, they sigh and look away
from the bosom by Rubens under the shirt by Sportsgirl,
and that smile by da Vinci, half-innocent of it all.

Ice-Oh!

Although we loved the gentle horse whose nose
of tired velvet nudged us for rye-grass,
Antarctica come to the suburbs was what drew
us through the heat to trot beside his slow
and straining bulk or swing on the creaking cart:
only the ice-man galloped – through each gate,
bent double over the hessian-cushioned block
that weighed him down the side, around the back
and in with never a knock, boots puddling mud
over lino, till clunked on the chest-edge to teeter and thud.
Hot-foot, hot-foot on the road we'd wait,
breathing the wet sack smell, the oats, the sweet-
sour yellow dung, force-feeding weeds to Horse
to earn our chunks of slithery dripping ice.
'Now clear off kids – and mind them bleedin' wheels.'
So perched on the fence we kicked our heels,
watching the cart lurch up to Duthy Street.
Johnny always waved as it turned right
and into just a faint clip-clop applause;
while fast as we could suck or slurp, our ice
was licked off at the corners by the sun
or sent in shivery runnels down our skin
trickling chocolate drops across the dirt.
And when we held the chips up glistening bright,
greyly among the frozen bubble swarms
there went a crooked mile between the palms
to question-mark the light. Beyond us, time
hung round on the wall; at every touch was home –
green streets, my brother's laugh, a sunny day,
only half-grasped, forever melting away.

JENNIFER RANKIN

I Had a Room

The room is still there
pale and glowing amongst the tall grass.

Once I closed the thick oak door
and the room broke itself off from the house.

Thousands of years ago.

The green-topped desk
still cluttered with papers and books
jiggles its weak leg under my moving wrist

and I am encompassed.
Even my shoe catches in that curl of worn carpet
that softly meets my urgent chair.

Outside there is a gale and springtime.
There is snow and bitter women
weeping through letters.
There is a children's party and a small girl
in a dress with a sash.

Inside out of my head
black rafters whirl away in long straight lines.
They support the roof of this room.
They bar the sky.

Tonight the room glows in the tall grass.
Someone is beckoning.
I bow my head
and a great bird flies hard against the page.

LEE CATALDI

Evening and all that Jazz

I dedicate this cigarette to you
like the other things you lit in my life
that are burning slowly down to the end

another time I would have become
a nun out of reach of the world

the world which fades
slowly with your face into this page

I would be safe from your return

but here which knows no haven
anything can happen

the sky can open and swallow you
before my astonished gaze

after a shipwreck debris floats
in the waves
I search in a disconsolate dinghy
for any sign of hope
light fades

like a patchwork quilt slowly sinking
the world fragments
into haze

SILVANA GARDNER

Shadow Ape

The first sighting occurred in a rain forest
of the Congo. Being a shy creature he hid
behind thick growth. All I could see
was his brown walnut eyes
and the remarkably manlike feet.
I said 'hello' forgetting the speech
rehearsed for such a meeting. Sounds
of crashing timber warned me he was fleeing.

I'm no longer part
of that expedition, having shifted
my interests on the psychic life of ants
(for which you never leave home)
but last Winter I saw the gorilla again
hiding behind the palm in the bathroom.
This time I was ready: so you've come back, have you?
No reply.
When did you get here? No reply.
It's difficult to communicate
with Western gorillas so I continued to part
my hair in the middle for a balanced look
thinking he'll talk when he wants to.

Obviously he has made my place his home.
Appears unannounced when I'm alone.
Perhaps I should feel privileged
but it's disconcerting when he doesn't speak.
I found a message in the garden,
hieroglyphs of twigs; one house: four sticks,
gorilla: one stick, me: one stone,
talk: sticks and stones. He could break my bones!

Now he's beginning to wear clothes,
adopts an air of *je ne sais quoi*!
I'm learning Esperanto to be ready
when he speaks. Last week he left
another message, cut-out letters

from the Courier Mail (he must've taken a course!)
Have you been to Havana?
Have you tried a kabana?
Is your name Silvana?

I don't like the way things
are progressing, his panama hat,
the pink Sobranies . . .
my telegram to him spelt
EAT MORE BANANAS!
He's getting on my nerves, hate the fashion
he wears, the plucking of his facial hairs
and today he was so close
I feared he wanted to play 'dares'.

He's lost all dignity! The city
has gone to his head! I call him *Castrone*!
and bet he'll never be my best friend,
he has learnt to V his fingers,
peace? Victory? Get nicked?

In the old days, any noise
would make him bolt so I leave music
blaring but now he sways to the rhythm
of anything, Bach, Debussy, Punk or New Wave
aping my ineptitude to dance. Throws tantrums
when I refuse to play 'have you been to Havana?'
Blows raspberries when I curse
'get lost in the lantana!'

To think I once loved gorillas, hoped
to rear one as a son . . . now this troop leader
shatters the aura of my working-class ants,
drinks my buttermilk, eats my nuts
and has learnt to spit all' Italiana.
There's no limit to his ambitions.
He's considering the role of a suburban Yeti,
tomorrow: the world! But I'm relying
on his initial shyness . . .
        My God, there he is!
                There he is!

COLLEEN BURKE

Why we didn't go away on the long weekend

Let us go away for the weekend he said
out of the city
                              into the high country
after all we went to england to see the snow
and didn't – you arrange it
rang up trains – waited 6 hours for some one
to say hullo – rang up again to enquire times/
                    bookings etc. meanwhile
governments rose/fell there were 2 coups, 1½
rebellions, a revolution – nearly – the
president died – long live the king.
                    Knowing we had to get up early
we stayed   up late   arguing.
                              Slept
beyond the alarm into morning   the train
went without us   full of imagination he
booked a plane.
                    Rang taxis to take
us to airport – no answer – they (the taxis)
          probably defected to russia/china.
                    Above
the city heard the plane singing   into the
high country and the sound of tourists   trudging
      into the snow   with cars
              o Kosciusko
for you they come   walking
                    At home with wet feet   sludgy
hearts   we sat around   a radiator
      hating   each other   slowly

Call Around and See Us

I am alone
the house is empty
                it breathes
& creaks like people
walking
slow
   the greeks next door
but one are having a barbeque
I hear them   through the
cracks singing   loudly
   they sound happy
   I stood for a while
   feeling the warm skin
   of the frangipani flowers
listening to them
falling dead around me
                  burning
the darkgrass   smelling   the music/
woodsmoke   sometimes the greeks and I say
   hullo but mostly we don't
   maybe we are shy   maybe
I sit here alone
          and think
of my men friends who criticise
my writing for being too personal
whatever that means
               ah I know
and ever since I can remember I
strove to be depersonalised – did you?
   I dressed in
dark interesting colours avoided
sunlight   rarely spoke
never 'lost' my 'irish' temper
sometimes smiled
             mostly hovered
sometimes thought of suicide

mostly hovered
                 passive
                      invisible
watching others act
                      & refraining
myself   invisible
sometimes looked obliquely
through windows & doors and people
called me efficient
                      fallen flowers singe
the darkness   the petals are   warm
like skin   i still have my   role
   my invisibility
but changed older different
   I am uneasy
in these close fitting garments
   and to my male friends
I say
   I will talk about you me us
women
   I will drag us out of cupboards
expose us   because we are personal
dark burning flowers of madness   alive
alone together   and   we are
going to criticise you   your world
   say our clothes are too small
and that the house
is empty and has always been empty
   and we say to you
look at yourselves (if you have the guts)
   call around and see us
   but we are going out

I Feel Lousy

Have you ever had one of the social
diseases
i caught one myself recently
rashes   along   the neck
for a week didn't notice   just
scratched   happily away   patience
i have been told is one of my better
characteristics   then   i felt a lump
behind the ear   cancer   off i go
to the doctor   just a rash   he said
what about the lump   your lymph
glands are infected   lovely name that
one more medical term   to throw around
amongst lay people   gave me a prescription
or two what's $4.00 between friends   smiling i
go back to work   still scratching away
saw this thing on my hand   a tiny revolting
insect   rang my doctor   lice he said   mine
were fully grown louses   applying for the
old age pension i'll refer them to the
social worker   lice every hair on my body
packed its bag and started running   i'm
not even english shower every day and sometimes two
– me? – rush down to nurses get disinfectant
anything to kill the bastards even gelignite
i am a passivist but you've got   to fight
these things.   Got a health commission
pamphlet which assured me there is no social
stigma attached to lice anyone can get them
nothing to do with me   probably the dirty
kids at the local school or the old man
who sat next to me on the bus the other day.
Well i must say it felt funny not being alone
no longer an alienated product of
capitalist society
all those little creatures living off me what
with inflation and all   didn't know my wages

could go so far   they are bludgers   will
report them to the Minister for Social Security
they are probably male chauvinists to boot
just my luck.   Sat in on a university lecture
when the genteel lecturer said on page 116
of ye olde manuscript what do you think
the hero is doing sitting naked in the snow
and picking things off his clothes – could
think of several things but we all looked
blank   lice he said   of course we don't
get them in this nice western society of ours
my god if he could see my hair more overcrowded
than wynyard at peak hour – a colony of lice –
wonder if they have a governor general –
perhaps charles would like the job   anyway
went home washed everything hair sheets people
hung them on the line to dry.

My hair is itchy

again don't tell me the bastards are back.   This
time i'll go to the chemist and get some ddt
what's good enough for the vegies is good
enough for me by the way it is highly
infectious and makes you feel lousy

ALEXANDRA SEDDON

Mornings : 3

an old morning
from a nest under a diamond mirror
the cold dark
outside a new calf baaing hungry
inside I am searching for socks and a jumper
sometimes I wear only coat and gumboots
easier to find in the dark
two crimson buckets and one brown bucket
hanging above the sink
slightly to the right
one sweep of the arm takes the brown bucket
off its hook and lowers it into the sink
the hot tap runs into it
one third full
another sweep of the arm takes the other two buckets
these gestures have been rehearsed so often that
there is no need to wake up properly
out through door
out through gate
into shed
some oats in tin and brown meal
smells like porridge warm
the cow pushing past me settling down
dark clouds and a bright sun through a hole in them
the light surreal like an eclipse
    I remember how the hens ran as they do at night
    to the hen house when the eclipse came and
    emerged an hour later when the light came back
yawning squeezing out the milk gently
the song beginning again in my head:
it's just an old war not even a cold war

CAROLINE CADDY

Lenny

i

I never got on with my father.
He had these sayings
like   dont do as I do just do as I tell you to do.
My mother was always telling me if I didnt mind
he'd whip me.
And he'd come home and you never knew when he was coming
and I had to take my pants down and get over his knee –
on my bare can   just like that.

First time I came to her house was on a Sunday
and they were all round the table.
It was like I never saw a family before.
To be there all at once with the mother
and the father and all these children
around the table
and to hear them make a prayer –
boy I tell you
I thought it was the greatest thing in the world.

ii

I wasnt making any money. I couldnt pay nothing.
I was making nothing no matter how much I sold.
My ulcers were bleeding and I didnt even know I had them.
That's when I decided to get out.
So I get my tools again   you know   woodwork.
And I just go round and say   you need any work done?
I walked miles   goddam miles.
Then someone says   yeah I got a job.
Then a couple more   couple more.
I changed. I calmed down.
I found I could sell myself. They liked me.

I have strong feelings.
I like to touch.
She's more reserved and I respect that
but sometimes I feel Jesus honey hug me
sit on my lap.
There's this picture
it got double exposed –
this tree growing right up out of her
twigs and veins all over and coming out.
She thinks it's a mistake but I think it's beautiful.
It's my favourite.

BOBBI SYKES

Black Woman

Black Woman
        your near meat-less stew
        boils over in the kitchen
        you stand at the front door
        your baby in your arms
        next youngest twisting at your skirts
        you listen to the man
        from the Australia Party
        asking you to become a candidate
        in the forthcoming election
         – in your hand today's mail
        advising you of scholarship benefits
        and black medical services
        your mind wanders to johnny
        lying in the back room
        wheezing his tiny life away
        and to the two you lost before
        the advent of black services.

Black Woman
        the electricity bill is not paid
        but the churches now court your attention
        you are asked to speak to groups
        in your st. vincent de paul dress
        but all the attention paid
        to your mate serving
        his ninth prison sentence
        for breaking and entering the homes
        of whites in the dead of night
        to gather crumbs
        to bring to your poor home
        does not set him free
        or put him back in your arms
        nor let you look into his eyes
        for one minute longer than 'visiting hours'.

Black Woman

>the present is so un-real
>its new *l* - liberal views
>mouthing anti-racist slogans
>in demonstrations of the day –
>attempting to solicit your sexual favour
>for a dollar and a drink
>in the cold reality of night
>you wonder if you were better off
>before the trendy 70's
>when you could stir your meatless stew
>think of wheezing johnny
>the un-paid bills
>without interruptions from the new world
>that promises much but delivers little

Black Woman

>the tears you cry – you are told –
>should be tears of joy
>black women are on the way '*up*'
>you now must ponder
>who will babysit the kids
>while you make your (un-paid) t.v. appearance
>you must try not to let your bitterness
>be construed as 'black racism'
>as you recall the abuses
>heaped upon you all your life
>and you view your 'liberation'
>with a scepticism born of poverty,
>corrugated-iron shacks, no water,
>four children from six live births
>and the accumulated pain of two centuries

black woman black woman black woman black woman black

from Love Poems

I
like the look of you/
moving easily in the street/
                stopping to notice the clouds/
                            the flowers/
                            the cut-price clothes
in store windows;
Eyes slipping stealthily sideways
to catch your own image in the windows/
                        as you pass
to make sure you look
as good as you feel.

I noticed you yesterday/too/
            and a time or two before that/
But then/
        I was in haste/
        doing my thing/
And you just flashed into my mind and vision
                    looking *GOOD*
But today/
        you look good/
                and available.

CHRISTINE CHURCHES

My Mother and the Trees

She shook the doormat free of dogs,
struck the tank to measure water, as she
marshalled us with iron buckets
to carry rations for the trees.

From fibres of air, she wove
us there the hope of leaves,
and in the flat and tepid dust
she dreamed a dwelling place of shade.

Summer by summer we carted water, slopped
lopsided up and back across the paddock:
the promised land a skeleton of stakes and hessian,
her voice insistent that they lived.

Reluctant slaves and unbelievers,
we sat out of sight
with our feet in the buckets, as she
filled the sky to the brim with trees.

STEFANIE BENNETT

Union Jacks

To all believers everywhere I am part of your barnyard.
I refuse to be perfect. I'm no / cool bold baby – I reject
the literary bib. I'll swap no spoon nor keep
forecasts. I'll not write the kind of lullaby, the one
set to hold wolves at bay.
I guess you could say, what use, what earthly
measure breaks bread with such hot air? Other
glad/bags of air & their country cousins, that's who.

Anyone of you leaning towards what I may
trip across & choose in the name of truth: Charity
begins where hope lets go, so, where's it lead? Let's be fair.
I'm not in love with my style, my flair. I don't honestly
believe I lay claim to either.
Gentlemen! Ladies! My striptease. I won't please; I'll
most likely yawn or sneeze & always
but always in the wrong places. Why, you
could fall for this act if I didn't play serious
more often than is good for me. That's it. You surely

heard me right. We grow tired of winners. The wild
has a way of greeting what's stacked against us.
I say 'us', it has a familiar ring. We've met before
when I was doing my number else you were doing yours.
Could it be we called an encore a draw? Now you're getting
there, see! How we prop each self up.
Fact is, a slave is a slave. It takes one to –
& am I not clever being on the outside, the offside; I mean
just consider the field this time round?

Some'll give you sonnets & some know the dance of darkness
& some will yank your entrails you'll think
you've the clap: Weak knees. I suffer them. I freeze
at the thought—; this: It could well be
my last testament. I'd best imagine it if I'm to continue
to convince I'm on the Up & Up. While we're about it let's

kid just a mite further down the gardenpath.
The vibrato of the barn yard: Remember I met you some
38 lines back? I could've preened it, I could've
crowned us in metaphor. Come on now, who & what revival's
kissing the clover, whose straw are
we sipping, name the place we've moved over for. Sleight
of hand! An eye: An eye. Give me more details & stump
    it further.

Brethren we are gathered here today –
holy Ghosts & Pentecost.
Each of us mount some trough, each of us because
    Poets' Officialdom's what I'm bludgeoning at. The hay
could've been greener: I've been meaning to write you about
    this.

JOANNE BURNS

real land

this must be the fifth bloody time this month ive spent the
day sittin in this corridor. its a real cold hole deadset.
might as well be in Siberia. as if theyd care all them jerks
of teachers sittin with their bums on top of the heaters in the
classroom all day. she said that Miss Lovall i'm putting
you out here near my office for your own good Cheryl.
yeah i say theres no need to bung it on i get the picture.
that will be enough she said Cheryl. here is a book of maps
for you to draw. this will keep you busy. i want you to
complete the first ten maps before lunchtime. you might
learn something. at least when you're holding your pen
you might be able to hold your tongue. she goes back to
her office. and ive been sittin here for ages at this grotty
little table and wobbly chair. shell be real tickled when
she sees i'm only up to map three. can't hack all these squiggles
and lines and all this kindergarten colourin in. real land
doesn't look like this who ever heard of pink and blue earth.
might smarten up this joint 'ere on the map with a bit of me
Orange Tropical Glow nail polish – just touch up this bit
'ere round the Cape of Good Hope. then i'll put a bit of
purple eyeshadow 'ere on Antarctica – brighten it up a bit –
sounds like a dag of a place to me – all that ice. all these
countries strange bloody words they got for names some of
these places. must be queer or somethin. this maps stuff
is too neat for me sissy stuff – like making cakes and sewin
classes. all that dumb embroidery. little chickens on
aprons for mumsie on Mothers Day. makes you wanna
spew. come on Cheryl Mrs Cotton used to say you could
stitch nicely if you try. look lady i said to her ive already
got six stitches on me chin from when i jumped and fell out
of the Dentention Room in Primary school. i know as
much about stitches as i'll ever need to know.

gees this place gives me the creeps all them teachers wierdos
thinkin they know whats best for you when half the time

they dont even know how to spell yr name right.   who are
they trying to kid.   and when they played detectives trying
to find out who set fire to the dunnies last week.   old 4 eyes
had to look up the roll to see who was in his class.   really
on the ball that jerk.   just wait till i get me hands on that
little punk Dwaynie Dickson for dobbin' me in. it was him
who gave me the matches.   got me a 2 day suspension and
now i'm sittin in this bloody corridor.   he'll be packin it
when i get 'im.   anyway they never found who burnt the
toilet rolls in the garbage bins.   geeze it made a good blaze.

i cant hack some of the guys in this school.   when they hang
in a group they act like Superman.   but get them by themselves theyre as weak as bubble gum. think theyre really
spunky calling us girls moles – if anyone says that to me i
just walk up to them between the eyes and say look here jerk
if you call me a mole again youll grow warts at the end of
your tongue.

wonder what the time is – i'm getting sick of this.   guess its
better than writing lines like i had to when i tried to grab my
jewellery back out of old Fowlers bag. i must keep my hands
to myself one thousand times.   jesus that wasa bastard.   she
had no right to take me silver marijuana leaf charm and me
Sid Vicious badge.   she didnt buy em.   jeez it was funny
when we were both pullin at her bag in front of the History
class and the handle snapped and everything fall out on to
the floor.   the things she had in her bag.   must have been at
least 20 old photos.   must carry all her past round with her.
no wonder shes a history teacher.

when i get out of this place therell be no more dumb books
for Chezza. i'll please myself, do what i like.   no washin'
nappies and listenin to babies cryin like me sister Fay.
20 year old and she looks like a hag with them brats a kids
and that slob of a guy shes married to.   never has a moment
to herself. naw.   i'm gonna be free.   travel round and see
real land.   not maps in books, travel round in me own
wheels.   not gonna have any boss breathin down me neck all
day.   think i'll be a semi-trailer driver.   out on the road
with me tranny. ridin high in the cabin wearin what i like.

i'll be good.   got good eyesight.   could drive me brother's
Falcon when i was eight.   took it out for a spin while he was
mowing the lawn one day.   dunno what all the fuss was
about.   i could drive better than all them jerks you see on
the road crawlin along like they was sleepwalkin.   yeah i'll
get me licence real easy no risk.   then one day i'll have me
own truck.   Chezzas Transport Company.   yeah, you'll
see all youse teachers –

    ooley dooley
    Cheryl Cooley
    she's no fooley

stacking it/another suicide
on the death of Anne Sexton

and so the poet, spluttering potential
accepts her clot/ignites the requirements
and motors into death:
          Muse has no more gears to steer
          her into one more poem, the empires
          of illusion
               Dido knew the logic
               behind pyres

          each death has its own
          dimension/the carefully
          fashioned wardrobe; bridges
          and ovens, rivers and General
          Motors Ford
               make special claims
               insist their policy's
               paid up/demand divine
               passage into metaphor
               the rising crime of
               legend, the public
               library shrine

and so the poet passes over
in her prime/'her newest DEATH NOTEBOOK
is the most alive' the blurb assures
but the camera cannot lie, those
Bedlam eyes already halfway back
beyond the Book of Folly

        and after the three days
        deep into dawn will
        some Saviour rise and resurrect
        the snoring secrets for
        biographers to serialize

            how many meanings
            can one prescription hold

            how many volts can shock
            give to its metre

            how many stanzas
            can therapy inspire?

the publishers will telegram invitations
to the reviewers' spies/
        so Literature survives . . .

she had more friends
than you could fit
into the back of a truck

that's why she didn't mind
leaving them parked
on a cliff edge

while she went
for a stroll
with the brake in her pocket

from Pillows

reading

there were so many books. she had to separate them to avoid being overwhelmed by the excessive implications of their words. she kept hundreds in a series of boxes inside a wire cage in a warehouse. and hundreds more on the shelves of her various rooms. when she changed houses she would pack some of the books into the boxes and exchange them for others that had been hibernating. these resurrected books were precious to her for a while. they had assumed the patinas of dusty chthonic wisdoms. and thus she would let them sit on the shelves admiring them from a distance. gathering time and air. she did not want to be intimate with their insides. the atmospherics suggested by the titles were enough. sometimes she would increase the psychic proximities between herself and the books and place a pile of them on the floor next to her bed. and quite possibly she absorbed their intentions while she slept.

if she intended travelling beyond a few hours she would occasionally remove a book from the shelves and place it in her bag. she carried 'the poetics of space' round india for three months and it returned to her shelves undamaged at the completion of the journey. every day of those three months she touched it and read some of the titles of its chapters to make sure it was there. and real. chapters called house and universe, nests, shells, intimate immensity, miniatures and, the significance of the hut. she had kept it in a pocket of her bag together with a coloured whistle and an acorn. she now kept this book in the darkness of her reference shelf. and she knew that one day she would have to admit to herself that this was the only book she had need of, that this was the book she would enter the pages of, that this was the book she was going to read

JERI KROLL

from Towers of Silence

BOMBAY

The Parsees*

The shadows circle back and out of sight.
Below, the priest unlocks the park.
The dead above lie open to the light.

The relatives have spent the night
listening to the dogs of memory bark.
The shadows circle back and out of sight.

The Parsees bury grief, they slight
the sleepless worm, the quick, efficient spark.
The dead above lie open to the light.

Keep earth and fire pure. It's right
to strip the soul to sail up to the ark.
The shadows circle back and out of sight.

Keep good and evil pure. Their flight
from Persia kept them choosing: light or dark.
The dead above lie open to the light.

The Towers silence vultures' wings. Their height
echoes with the skeleton's remark.
The shadows circle back and out of sight.
The dead above lie open to the light.

* part one of a longer poem

Bushfire Weather

It's cool in the hills,
breezes dart through houses like trapped birds
beating glass till they're free.
It's clean up there. Smog doesn't rain
across the garden, smudging the birds of paradise,
fingerprinting the windowsills.

It's calm in the hills when the frenzied heat
in the town bullies pedestrians.
The north wind eggs it on:
cotton wrapped like a second skin
loosens and billows, even sunglasses can't screen the grit,
the earth in the driveway's blown off,
vegetables wilt in the garden,
the city lies down like an old dog.

In century heat, in the tinder-dry hills,
air has an edge, too, but shade is kinder.
Children swing across the Onkaparinga
into cool green slime. Cats pant under water tanks,
horses munch prickly grass under rattling trees.

By one o'clock the city has a compress on its head,
no longer looks at the hills
as if they meant afterlife.
The north-east wind dries sweat running down the spine,
belches out yellow clouds, pummeling cyclists,
rocks the lucky sheep trucked from the hills.
Down in the mall the dogged buskers play
till a string snaps.

THUY AI NGUYEN THI

The Quôc Bird*

Coming back, I follow the old path
Weeds cover the way where there used to be flowers
A thousand clouds accompany me,
insist on walking me to that mountain.

The small bird gets woken,
shaken from the deep of a gold dream.
Listening to footsteps on the damp ground, he thinks
raindrop? tears?

Clouds fly to the north, home
and back to the south, home.
O how divine the original stream
opening this land's flowers, continuing
the ancestors' dreams.

Look at the flowers in the wind
and drifting on the surface of the water.
Now, earnestly comes the call from the bird
the distant sound of the quôc

calling flowers back to their old branch
calling cloud to mountain
calling bird to warm nest
calling me back to myself.

* In Vietnam in legendary times, a king lost his land and went into exile. It is said that when he died his soul returned in the form of the quôc bird. In the Vietnamese language, quôc means 'homeland'.

[translated from Vietnamese by Dao Nguyen and Susan Hampton]

RHYLL McMASTER

A festive poem

Balanced precariously on the backs of chairs
tacking awkwardly strung together Christmas cards
to the pelmet,
with thumbs feeling like pressed-out putty
and the kids scrambling,
squealing   'We can touch the ceiling!'

The time of the year we damn auntie
for her 'thought that counts' gift of gussies
untimely opened;
and brightly choke
our stunted sheoak with tangled lights
only to see them bad-connectedly go
phftt.

Time we make the drunken fruit mince
and rub flour into the calicoed pudding
knowing all the while we'll be too hot to eat it

tomorrow . . .

sitting on the beach
with sandflies on our silver hair-bleached arms
we say listlessly,
'It doesn't really feel Christmassy.'

LARAINE ROCHE

Wanderings

'What do you think those big balloony things are the
ballerinas are carrying?' asked Sidney,

'Probably tu-tu bags,' I said, leaning over the Opera
House rails to get a better look, 'They all look so fresh,
their parents look tired,' I stated. The darkness of the
harbour was powdered with decorative light bulbs around
the walking area. Some mini ballerinas giggled as they
held their small silver trophies close to their chests.' Their
hair was piled up like debutantes.

'I suppose you wish you hadn't married me, maybe
instead of being my wife you could have been a dancer or
a surgeon, you always wanted to continue medicine,'
Sidney's chin was silhouetted, trembling,

'That's not true, I like being your wife' I said. One of
the little wood nymphs had left her vanity case behind
and flitted into the shadows, her mother's voice imitated
a pelican.

'You knew it wouldn't be wine and roses when you
married me, I told you I didn't have a degree, or a skill,
I'm no good with my hands, definitely not a socialising
wit, if you want to leave me just say the word,' Sidney
gasped. In the Opera House coffee shop, the waiters were
stacking chairs in tight fitting tuxedos, goldfish under
glass.

'I told you I don't want to leave you, I'm happy with
you' I said, he was trembling 'You're not too cold are
you?'
'No,'
'I think ballerinas were born ballerinas, they're all so thin
and tall, but that hairdo makes them a few inches taller.
Where do they all go after the show? Maybe they sit
around at someone's house and discuss the inflated price

of shoe powder. Maybe someone offers one a cake and
she says "No thanks, I'm playing the Dying Swan next
week and have to keep my weight down"' I said, lighting
one of Sidney's Viscounts.

'Who was that Martin character you said hullo to in the
supermarket yesterday? I wouldn't blame you if you
were seeing someone else, the hours I've been working
at the shop lately, I'm too tired to do anything when I
get home,' Sidney had one of his famous pouts on.

'Martin used to go out with a friend of mine, but why
should I take a lover? I understand how tired you must
be, housework's pretty exhausting too.' I said, as Sidney
feverishly grasped my free hand,
'Is there anything that, well, you want to tell me?'
he said, 'Shit, Sidney, what are you going on about,
why are you so insecure lately?'

'I'm sorry, my nerves are all shot what with the car
repayments doubling, but I can't afford a holiday,'

A security guard was heading our way and we began to
walk back to the car. Most of the ballerinas and assorted
relatives had disappeared into the night with their bags of
gossamer and lace. The last of the greyhound buses
galloped homeward.

'Did you have a good night? Maybe when the tax cheque
comes in we could go to the ballet, we'll see eh?'
'Sure' I answered stubbing out my cigarette in the
ocean.

The dancing lessons started that week.

CAROL NOVACK

You try to get out of the fear

you try to get out of the fear
by going into it

like quicksand it holds you
like a mother it will not let you
go

all year long you woo it
like a father it tells you to keep on
for one day you will marry it

all year long you swallow it
in doses large enough to knock
even buffalo bill off his high
horse
and develop your aims
as good as annie oakley you are
shooting straight into yourself

you take it like a soldier
drafted into the fear
pinions you into various positions
you take it and it takes you
lying down wearing strange faces
oddly alike and always in the dark
removed by mornings it comes
relentlessly and too fast

so you try riding it
like a taoist colt but it won't budge

and you try marrying it
you cover its windows with beige
curtains to soften the glare
and make sacrifices to it
but it laughs like Moloch
its eyes gleaming like new sterling silver

so you try divorcing it but it trails you
like a snakey shadow it is your mother again
and places warning signals
on the roads

one day when you least expect
it goes maybe on vacation
and you wonder where it will turn up
next

The Staircase

I

I am sitting on a staircase. Below me, steps rise and fall. Above me, the pattern repeats itself. I am a figment of my own imagination. I pinch myself.

The room around me, down the stairs and to the right is full of green couch. And the one window which hides a fence which attempts to hide the next house (which is probably constructed of green couch) is clothed in brown velvet.

If you were to sit on the couch there you'd be facing a black and white picture of an impossible edifice, a water mill constructed of three levels separated by pillars. Look again. The water flows into itself and the three levels are one level. Next to the mill is another smaller building with a terrace on which a woman is hanging clothes. And beyond the mill are steppes, stairs of crops that don't exist. The woman looks comfortable among abstractions.

The people on the couch, surrounded by earth colours, are also comfortable among abstractions of earth. Lips move up and down, voices rise and fall up and down the steps.

The green couch was there before I came to inhabit the house, but I accepted it. I am filling it with gestures.

When the last notes of the chorus descend into night we will make our way up the stairs and sleep like two felled trees that have accidentally touched one another on their way down.

We will sleep.

II

You asked me what it was like, being married, and I told you it was
like sitting on a staircase, below me the steps rising and falling.
Above me, the pattern repeated itself and I rested like a slow
intermission.

The room around me, down the stairs (if you're inclined to literal
motion) and to the right was full of green couch. If you sat on the
couch – I used to invite people into my marriage and they'd sit on the
couch, surrounded by earth colours, also comfortable abstractions of
earth. Lips moved up and down, voices rose up and down the steps.
This was my landscape.

The green couch was there before I came to inhabit the house but it
was accepted. I filled it with gestures. When the last notes of the
chorus descended into night we'd make our way up the stairs. Felled.
Accidentally touching.

In time the house oppressed me so I'd say let's throw a party and
we'll cook exotic dishes. And let's paint one wall red and perhaps
another yellow.

And suddenly I wanted to fly out of, over, or into earth colours,
green couch – all the uncomfortable abstractions.

BEATE JOSEPHI

Tuscan Dream

For weeks they did nothing. They lay in hot rooms on whose
ceilings, at night, the streetlamps contrived strange patterns.
Lilies, moons, star-cores.

They read books whose expansive style embraced whole worlds
and
particularly their uncertainties. Read without dreaming. Outside
the landscape brooded. People scratched hay together, bundled it
into squares. Olives ripened, and grapes.

Motionless they lay in the upper rooms. The window showed
them
cloud at night, towards morning they saw fog over the river-bed.
At noon, the overclear landscape. No dreams, only details. A
landscape hiding its valleys and showing up distance only with a
paling of colour.

One morning they painted. Slowly they drew up pink walls and
battlements, banners waved from the tower. And in front of the
pale red walls they put tents. Beautiful striped tents with
golden piping and braids and tassels where roofs and sides met.
A mighty field of red and white stripes.

But there was dust around the tents, a martial glistening of
spears and lances. The dust of noon had caught up with them.
Soon
the shutters would have to be closed, the pot of basil shifted into
the shade.

In the half darkness of room and wine they designed the inner
courtyard. He put in a fountain carried by strong animal backs,
arranged tiles in intricate patterns. She brought fig and
pomegranate trees which grew with the falling of water until
their fruit would give in to ripeness and thud on the hot stone.
A revelation of the beauty of inner wounds.

They went up to their beds in the upper rooms. Lilies, moons,
star-cores: their Courtyard of Lions, their cloister, their
passion.

ANNA COUANI

Drawing The Fruit

the children draw the pineapple
and paint it yellow or orange
more simply and clearly than the other fruit.
they put in the fruitbowl
under the fruit but not around the fruit.
the fruit are on the bowl not in it.
they sweep through the classroom
which is quieter after they leave than before
and tidier.
they order things by uprooting everything
they put things where they should be
they don't leave them where they are.

What a man, what a moon

What a man, what a moon, what a fish, what a chip, what a block, w
a mind, what a tool, what a drive, what a car, what a tent, what a
pitch, what a scream, what a joke, what a suit, what a flash, what a
view, what a jump, what a pain, what an arse, what a tree, what a
trunk, what a boat, what a sea, what a blue, what a song, what a roo
what a jerk, what a pump, what a drink, what a mouth, what a guy,
what a doll, what a smash, what a hit, what a fight, what a fuck, wh
rock, what a ring, what a stone, what a jar, what a whack, what a ja
what a sheet, what a mess, what a room, what a crutch,
what a limp, what a walk, what a day, what a beach, what a swim,
what a bath, what a dog, what a cow, what a pig, what a snort, wha
trip, what a shot, what a grape, what a wine, what a glass, what a cu
what a lip, what a hand, what a foot, what a lawn, what a gnome, w
a pet, what a fit, what a bum, what a heel, what a nail, what a bash
what a phone, what a dial, what a tooth, what a drill, what a screw,
what a ball, what a clinch, what a dick, what a bind, what a scene,
what a smoke, what a dive, what a splash, what a height, what a clif

The Train

You show me your child. You're standing so close to me,
whispering. I can feel the hard material of your harsh black
suit and your bony elbows underneath it. You are controlled.
You look controlled. You're about to tell me the tragedy. We
look at the child with dark eyes and dark hair. I look at
your wife standing behind you. She's blind. This must be the tragedy.
I grab your elbow out of pity. The wife and now the
child. But you smile and say, No, the child can see – isn't she
beautiful. The child isn't tragic, you and I are tragic.

You keep talking. You can't run away from the past. You carry
your memories with you always. This is something you say when
you expect remorse and penitence from me. You want to see me
as the escapee with the head wounds. Scarred by love and still
limping. Childless and alone.

The sun streams into the room through the doors onto the
balcony. I sleep for days and days to forget. I dream about
the train where we all lived together. You said the train
always stands for the past. Our homes were the carriages joined
together. The train stopped outside the town in the countryside.
We jumped off and ran around in the long grass shouting and
laughing. One man set a fire through the train and burnt all the
unnecessary things. A purification. You can't run away from the
past, you said. I tried to light the fire but I didn't have the
knack. I burnt the blue chest of drawers and scorched the timber
panelling. Only one person could light the fire correctly. He
was the escapee who never felt remorseful or penitent. He was
always forgiven and never carried the past with him.

But if the train was all our houses joined together from the past
and through the present into the future, the train is not the
past but our lives as they run together. And the man who changed
our lives without destroying us has gone away and taken his secret
with him. You stand beside me now, more gentle than you've ever
been because you're relieved that the kid didn't have to carry our
own afflictions.

The Map of the World

The map of the world is felt from the inside. Rough around the
coastlines and smooth over the hills and sand dunes. Warm and moist
through the rivers which lead outside to the forests like long hair
then sparser like shorter more bristly hair to the touch. Reading a
globe of the world with its topography in relief. Reading with the
fingers as though blind. Feeling it with the back, down the spine.
Making contact with the nipples and the nose only. Moving at a fast
rate underwater through the oceans and large lakes. Most of the
oceans connect up with each other. Moving so fast that you become
aware of the earth's surface being curved. Flying low but fast across
the land masses. Make yourself feel like the world. As old but not
as troubled.

We could smell the salt in the air at Parramatta
That was where the city began in those days
Then everything had a kind of sameness until we hit the city
Everything seemed old and dirty, running beside the tram tracks.
Newtown seemed particularly old and Redfern not at all red or fern-like
This was one idea of old, but not like the mountains which were ancient

And in between this old and this ancient was European old and the
                                        ancient
Of the Mediterranean and Asia.   But I didn't know that, it was a blan
                                        for me like Parramatta
Was till recently. And I never thought I'd find people I could like
Not in the enduring way I loved the mountains and the city, where day
Counted for nothing against 'forever'. Bush love like bush tracks
And city love I could trace back to Sydney's birth as a city.

My memories are my grandma's memories of the city
And my mother's talks looking at the mountains, talking about
                        The Ancient
About the beginning of the world like a 2001 movie track
But more serious. And Dad feeling alien anywhere west of Parramatta
Or Broadway even. I felt his sense of relief on the days
We came down to the city and he showed me what his Sydney was like

Where we saw salami and olives in shops I now realize were just like
Ones in Greece and definitely unlike the big Franklins in the city
Which sold DEVON (a word my parents pronounced like POISON).
There were different city days
With Mum, more anglo. Sitting in the Cahills coffee shop looking at the
ancient
Egyptian motifs etched on the amber mirrored walls.   Stopping at
Parramatta
For a sandwich and having a talk about the Great Western Highway
when it was just a track.

Just as Mum knew the mountain tracks, Dad knew the city tracks
Not just the steps and pathways around the Cross for example, but he had
a mental picture like
A map. The shortcuts all the way from the coast to Parramatta
Which makes me think of Sydney as like a middle-eastern city
Multi-layered and only really knowable by people with that ancient
Knowledge which is still applicable in the cleaned-up version of Sydney
these days.

I had a dream of finding parts of Sydney I'd forgotten and rediscovered
on summer days
In the dust and heat. Suddenly finding a lane like a track
Leading between some buildings. But that's ancient
History to me now, that personal approach to writing. Now I like
To write about the things happening around me not to me. About the
city.
And I want to start from the centre I know and work outwards past
Parramatta.

Even trying to avoid nostalgia, my childhood days
Seem ancient and thinking about them is like archeology
Tracking down connections and making them
Till they stand out as strongly and clearly as the arterial roads
Between the city. Parramatta and the mountains.

VICKI VIIDIKAS

Four poems on a theme

Inside of Paradise

We are coming and going. At last you have arrived, your suede shoes like soft faces brushing the floor. Advertising, you say, recognising your face stacked on a library shelf. The thrushes have left the eaves. You are alone inside the tower, respected, working. An elm knocks on the window. I come in wearing blood, a cloak edged from outside. How many times must I walk this threshold? You swivel saying, I have lost Paradise, I thought I was done.

I am bringing you rain and African deserts, animals in need of shelter. We are arriving in a circle, we are coming through cultures and lost continents, sometimes I don't know what to tell you. Act, I think, I never know where to begin. You fall away a glass paperweight, a faded map of lost Peru. I am a stranger in your drawing room, want to take you outside. I say, these are the knives, take one in pledge. You have a history to reject as I recreate idols. Voodoo men own my laughter, they have a claim on me like you. The shaman is out to get you, make you jangle inside of Paradise. Chaotically we're arriving. This time the risk is gold.

I have your feather, I never forget.

A Trunkful of Structures

Daylight hasn't entered this library. Beaded fluorescent lights shine like dominoes on the ceiling. Traffic is steadily flushing its own purpose down the street. No good, you say, meaning I do not fit into your life. No good. The streets are full with animals carrying sharp sticks, handbags, cruel eyes. It's the beginning of another week and we're all moving into familiar patterns. You must keep your car repaired, you who never risk buses.

I am stalking a zebra crossing, lunchtime crammed with shoppers and stale sandwiches. I am in a library, my feet up on a chair. Great Lives, Great Men and Great Words confront me. I don't even flinch. Curtains keep the sun out, readers have fallen asleep in chairs. I am among the shelves looking for a book. I am rummaging among the shelves searching for a word. You're nowhere in sight. And I'm looking for something. Not perfection or great lies. Not complicated gestures. Something to replace your strained eye. You're out of control. And books are leaning posts. These days it's hard to conjure up devils when there's only an hour for lunch.

I've never been in this library with you. Or in a pool room, or on a zebra crossing. I've been in bed with you, kissed you and wanted to draw blood. I imagine that is significant. That I have been in bed with you. That it was you and not a ghost. I imagine I can recognise, claim you, have you in my sensibility. Dream of fire and water and symbols to bind us together. But I can't.

Not you or anybody. I can acquaint myself with the edges of lives, read the intimate journals of some great writer. Tell others about you. Know it won't be you or anyone I'll spend 30 years of my life with. And the books are saying, believe, believe me. I exist. You exist. Readers adrift in dreams exist. Separately. So long into death. Into memories of your eye, 'how it was', the quarrels we never meant to have. My sagging bed, 'our romance', 'our affair'. The bridges you'd built and the water flowed under them. Each of us seeking belief thinking, I am significant. Want no more lies. Loved us away from structures, the closest thing to being free. Made us scent each other's blood. Away from tired defences. So we believe.

It's not true. You have dragged your ghosts with you, unable to fob them off. You've come rattling a trunkful of structures saying, here, try this one, perhaps it will fit. Like hats or shoes. They didn't. So you feel let down. Having my own trunk, and a sagging bed with a cat for a hot waterbottle. You've gone off wearing the old coat saying, no good. The structures like clamps. Leaving me to mine. Each of us squeezed breathless.

It's Natural

It's not enough, looking at you blundering like a turtle against the stream. Prowling my room like caged animals. Mud slinging. Nothing more violent than turning the eye in like a knife. I see. Fingerfuls of affection falling away like flesh. I imagine what her bed is like. You dropping into her like a well, forever lost, bottomless. Another territory.

Madness is in your eye. I want to carry you off and say yes, I've something more than a bed of straw. Yes, you're a coward, want to blow you up with words. Got a match? I can't replace you. I'm saying there's more to life than love. Eh? Yeah. Words. Structures.

The man in the communist bookshop was a capitalistic pig. Personally. And I say I've set up my affections like tin gods to be shot down. Absolutes. Wanting permanence. In and out of the line of vision. Fire. Essences. What more essence is there than your seed? Tomorrow night it could be in her. It's natural. I won't accept her. You? Tweed coat betrayer. Nonsense! I'm making a farce of it – this possessiveness, this claim. Removed from cities to mud huts. Honey I'm going to howl. Get your spear. It's my line.

Going Down. With No Permanence

I'm finding it impossible to begin, as you've ended so little. Last night my heart was a cheap flag waving to the nearest mirror in sight. I couldn't believe anything, seeing you drive away into others' arms. I'm no sweet virgin sock-washer either. So it's a matter of priorities I guess, just who wants to gamble. Talk of loving when there is no goal. Of belief when there is no road. My shoes are off and I'm walking barefoot. Down a long avenue of arms and kisses like knots. I'm getting tired and angry and thinking hell, I'm no sock-washer but there must be some other venue. I say my heart's big enough, it is. Every time it's eaten and collapses like a cough.

Today I'm trying to be reasonable. You're having breakfast with her. And there's no wedding ring, baby, fidelity, photo. No day to week token of what we have, a visible future. Crazy thing, it's happening everywhere. You waft into my room bringing delicious words, eyes, every other love you're still attached to, claim.

'I want all love-rites simultaneously.'

'I don't want to negate anything.'

Yes I understand. Incredible egotist! that one cracked heart is your own, gyrating in its uncertainty. Adoration. Adulation. Your heart seeks to reflect itself. Narcissus in the bath. How many loves do you want? Are you never full, leaky bucket?

And now you turn to your sock-washer reasoning socks are better than none. So you're surrounded again. Pursued and claimed. A shroud of outrage going up. Thinking of numbers and lines. It sharpens your humour. While I love this one the others must love me too. I'll keep my heart spinning. You think you're responding, keeping all the doors open. Yes. Yes.

This is the road my bare feet touch. Going down. The avenue with few affirmatives. Going down. With no permanence. This is the alternative to restrictions. So we assume. Without end.

Rehabilitation

Getting there always, the difficulty of sensation
and what its end result is, these lapses of confidence
and purpose / all experience yawning, wanting escape and
full abandonment, going off at high speed to some other
phased reality / wanting more, more . . .

Seeing the needle in your vein was a way of
reassuring myself, of what I didn't want, no half world
of shadows, yours and my blood mingling through a glass
syringe / I had to possess my little veins and know I
wanted them totally, not rushing with ecstatic juice,
not rushing to a world of nods, mumbles, aches, fevers
and the ice of coming down . . .

You see I've waded through this before, climbed
spikey fences, gone under ladders, skinned the black cat,
used voodoo and congolese mud to drive me towards the
sun / I couldn't turn back now, watch my shadow grow
mammoth and out of proportion, I couldn't carry this
burden and smell death in the closets again . . .

My veins carry red blood beautiful as it is, these
rubies of innate life, my body a house on earth / I've
found some unsown ground to plant these dream seeds in,
to sing, dance, sunbathe, imbibe the juices and sounds which
drift through trees and sky / either we keep the sun within
us, or our wings are bitter destroyers, taking us further
away . . .

PAMELA BROWN

One for Patti Smith

one of my friends lost her mind in nineteenth
century novels. i tried to have her take a cure.
i offered your books. i said here are wild dog hotel
poems. cocaine and cooked dog. i said. wild street.
totally present words. here take them they're for
you. read them now please.

once, my lover promised to fly you from new york.
on my birthday. i knew you'd find me tedious.
impervious to perversity. another day another fan.
my lover was full of empty promises and no money
anyway.

ps. i never had the ramones, stones, fabian forte or
anyone else on my wall.

The Red Cocacola Bottle

that we perform in syndicates
became obvious
when, while on weeks away
we found ourselves creating
some very unified notions

i spent the winter stoned
and decided on a pair
of gymboots

boiling up vermilion
in our workshops
to make a measure
on the world supply
of cocacola
and other works of heart;

desire in our dreams
and wistfulness.
all the time
i was wearing
the kind of shoes
that being alive
makes so dirty.

Honky Tonk Sunset

the chickens.

the guitar.

the chickenshit.

the lid
of the can
suspended
for the rifle.

the fence.

the chickens.

the guitar.

the chickenshit.

who is this guy
who walks into the house
with an immediate opinion
of herman hesse and advice
on how to cook the rice?

the longer i write poems for you
the shorter they become.

Leaving.

so now i have to pack my forests
    and baggages.
so now i have to pack my eagles
    and teardust.
and the way you talked to overflow.
and the way you were so fast to change
    into your many shades of sorrow.
and the way you swept the miracles
    away from your shabby gentility.
and the way you trembled
    as you chose the latest props.

so hello attache case face.
hello briefcase face.
hello screaming suitcase.

The Dear John Letter

between the sugar and the short black
something like grief   came over me

it was your cafe moralism.
from london to canada and back
to coaldust. lungs full of dead gymboots.
the cost of this and the cost of that.
the gold bands on white filtered cigarettes.

stranded there   enormous. sad.
grey   on the fringe of the neon.

in the bathroom
i noticed the dark rings under my eyes.
the deepening of the lines on my face.
the peoples palace towel on the rack.
                    in the bathroom
i remembered the only morning of my life;
                i sat on a tiled verandah
                with a woman in a blue kimono.
                small white boxes of coloured slides
                scattered around us.   i was
                holding the slides to the sunlight.

lately   every change
had scared and changed me.
through the bathroom window
a fat girl walked slowly over to a fountain.

i would rather kick and shout
        than grieve like that.

KATE JENNINGS

Couples

this is a song an epithalamium it is also
a requiem this is a poem about couples it
is called *racked and ranked*
the title comes from william faulkner
who said

'and thank God you can flee, can escape from that
massy five-foot-thick maggot-cheesy solidarity which
overlays the earths, in which men and women in couples
are racked and ranked like ninepins.'

this is a poem for couples from which i cannot escape
this is a poem for people who are not couples but who
want to be couples from which i cannot escape a poem
for all you out there people who are coupling up or
breaking up just to couple up again and giving me
second prize because

kate jennings, lose him, weep him, couldn't catch a man
much less keep him

couples create obstacle courses to prevent me from doing
all sorts of things easily
couples make sure i'm not comfortable with myself because
i'm only half a potential couple
couples point accusing right index fingers at me
couples make me guilty of loneliness, insecurity, or
worse still, lack of ambition.

what do i do at the end of the day?
lose him, weep him, think of catching a man,
and eating him.

One Kiss Too Many

'One kiss too many
And kisses lose their meaning'
Diane Wakoski

Let me, this once and without condemnation,
be churlish and openly maledictory
(my poetry might be a poetry of revenge
but having the last word is often pyrrhic):
I wish for you the loneliness
you have given me. I mean by loneliness not that
common state of being alone in a crowd,
but something else, more awful.

That is not nice of me.
I'm supposed to hug my grief and grievances
to myself and like an extraordinarily
benevolent peasant woman
wish you a long life, many offspring
and a multiplicity of happinesses. I should care
for you and keep the thought of you (you
as yourself I loved) precious
no matter where you go what you do
no matter where I go what I do.

Loving you has made me bitter and not
courteous or gracious or kind.
I did not learn about tenderness, warmth and
mystic moments of burning worlds and carnal satisfactions
(of which I've read in other people's poetry), although in my
fantasies I know of such things well
and tried to offer you a tenative self.

I cannot suffer fools gladly and
all men are fools (like the feminist
in *Miss MacIntosh, My Darling* I'll die
with forty trunks filled with bridal dresses).
I continue a petulant virago
and wish in my heart of hearts
that you will be weak, your ambitions thwarted,

and that you will be smitten with boils
until we know you not. And, unlike Job, you will not have
the integrity or wit to say
how long will you vex my soul,
and break me in pieces with words.

I fear my words and meanings are too simple,
my motives too transparent.
I will be fettered imaginatively and emotionally
if I cannot be more involved with matters other than
love has died, friendship has faded.
But because I loved you gladly
because we in a manner of speaking blew it baby
because I no longer like you
because I despise and curse you
and because I am lonely
I want to protest. I mean love's a myth isn't it.

EDITH SPEERS

Why I Like Men

mainly i like men because they're different
they're the opposite sex
no matter how much you pretend they're ordinary
human beings you don't really believe it

they have a whole different language and geography
so they're almost as good
as a trip overseas when life gets dull
and you start looking for a thrill

next i like men because they're all so different
one from the other
and unpredictable so you can never really know
what will happen from
looks alone

like anyone else i have my own taste with regard
to size and shape and color
but the kind of style that has nothing to do
with money can make you bet
on an outsider

lastly i guess i like men because they are the other
half of the human race
and you've got to start somewhere
learning to live and let live
with strangers

maybe it's because if you can leave your options open
ready to consider love
with such an out and out foreigner
it makes other people seem
so much easier

SUSAN HAMPTON

Yugoslav Story

Joze was born in the village of Loski Potok,
in a high-cheek-boned family. I noticed
he had no freckles, he liked playing cards,
and his women friends were calléd Maria, Malcka, Mimi;
and because he was a handsome stranger
I took him for a ride on my Yamaha
along the Great Western Highway
and we ate apples; I'd never met anyone
who ate apples by the case, whose father
had been shot at by Partisans in World War II,
who'd eaten frogs and turnips in the night,
and knew how to make pastry so thin
it covered the table like a soft cloth.
He knew how to kill and cut up a pig
and how to quickstep and polka. He lifted me up in the air.
He taught me to say '*Jaz te ljubim, ugasni luc*'
('I love you, turn off the light')
and how to cook *filana paprika, palacinka*,
and *prazena jetra*. One night in winter
Joze and two of his friends ate 53 *palacinke*
(pancakes) and went straight to the factory
from the last rummy game. Then he was my husband,
he called me '*moja zena*' and sang a dirty song
about Terezinka, a girl who sat on the chimney
waiting for her lover, and got a black bum.
He had four brothers and four sisters,
I had five sisters.
His father was a policeman under King Peter,
my father was a builder in bush towns.
Joze grew vegetables and smoked Marlboros
and he loved me. This was in 1968.

Stranded in Paradise

Your fuselage, your entourage,
your wingtip. now your eyes.
your feet which touch the ground.
stranded in Paradise
I'm climbing over your body
the hill of your breast
stranded. what god put me here.
my time with you. will you
kiss me again. like this. here.
now here. hold my head.
hold my feet down, I'm levitating.
it's so easy. when you roll over
onto me, I hold your fuselage.
I pat your wingtip. I touch your teeth
and your shoulders. you are sinking
into me. I balloon under your hand.
                              The night sky
is humming with crickets. and humming birds,
which only live in Paradise. which only exist
here. soon they will stop. the noises will stop
and we'll lie still. only the sound of the cars
and the clicking inside the metal boxes
for the traffic lights. someone slowing up
for a hitchhiker. and off again.
another person who'll be stranded.
will it be in Paradise, at the corner shop,
the fruit stall. will she hover over
the apples. delicious or jonathan.
she can't decide. it's because she's stranded,
and thinks it's only the fruit stall, or the corner shop.
it's only Paradise, I want to say. it's only here.
the planes going over. the traffic passing by.

Statues

Costumes

Certain types of costume immobilise the wearer, but this
reduction to a statue can be a form of magic. Everything rests
in potential. It means that anything can happen; all forms
of possible movement are included in the stillness. At any moment
a priest, an actor, a queen will move,
there is a noise, the play opens.

Opera

Do you remember Sutherland singing the part of the wind-up
doll in *The Tales of Hoffmann?* Partly alive and partly not,
the product of her maker's imagination. And how her lover couldn't
tell at first she wasn't real. Was that at the big concert in
the domain, or on TV? I remember thinking how wonderful the
story was, and the sound she made when she was winding down,

              ah

            a
              a
                a
                  a
                      aa
                        aa
                          a

Instructions on How to Release the Statues

The statues are made of marble or plaster. They sit or stand
or recline in the positions of Greek gods and goddesses. They
are waiting for someone to buy them. Diana and Apollo on Parramatta
Road. Do you want one in your garden?
   They hold each other's arms, or point to the birdbath or the
car yard across the road. Sitting in your car in the traffic
you suddenly notice them, a forest of muscular white limbs, a
theatre of profiles. Their ancient faces are holding pollution

in like grains of sand. The statues are all young. They are
ready to go. Do you want one? in your garden?

   They would like to be guarding the gates of the city. At the
entrance to the harbour. At Hornsby and Parramatta and Tempe.
At Arcadia. At Sylvania. A plaster shepherdess, draped with
ivy, holding a bowl of bougainvillea. But for now they are
trapped in the display area of Garden Artistry, watching the
Japanese cars accelerating towards the city, or towards the suburbs.

   Now to release the statues we take this key. Fit it to the mechanism
here at the small of the back. Try this statue. The
key turns easily. She walks away, lurching at first, walking
and falling, rising into the air. It is Winged Victory. She's
flying across the city. There she goes. Across the cars and
phonelines. All in white.

What is the Key?

Status? Is status the key? Is it consciousness? Is it the desire
for change? Will that flying woman land? Where will she touch down,
will she land too fast and break? Will someone catch her? Is she
hoping that? Or is she enjoying being up so high? Does she want
to come down? Where will she land? What is the key?

The Landing

Winged Victory touches down one evening
in the grounds of a mansion where a wedding is in progress.
All in white, with a partly raised arm, she is indistinguishable
from the other guests. After the ceremony she drinks champagne
and talks to a few lawyers and doctors,
mostly about sailing and shares. But *sailing* and *shares*
have changed their meaning. Her language is out of date.
Has she come down in the wrong part of town? She finds a
woman wearing a blue dress with white spots, who explains
how the public transport system works and lends her some
money. Winged Victory has begun her search, she is on a bus
to another part of town. There is a slight creak as she shifts
in her seat. She feels very old and at the same time new,
completely new.

JENNIFER MAIDEN

from The Trust
part one

                    As it is always said,
we-begin-here-at-the-end and anything which comes
after that is what we will discuss. Don't trust
me yet: I don't know what I will still
require of you, and you don't know
as yet the depth and danger in your trust.
There is no room here to run, and none
in you that I can run from. Here she is!
As always we display the woman first
and need some odds and ends, if just
hair-colour, eye-colour, length of breast
and length of fingernail. Her hair
is red, her eyes are white
as half-moons and her breasts are short
with parchment haloes. She's on the floor
somewhere in a stupour, but with no
suspicious pulse, no needlemark, no drama.
We don't need them. We can wake her.
When you do, you clasp her shoulders, fear
that somehow your hands don't look right,
don't look functional to me, since I watch
every caution entering between you. So
there isn't any kiss. Her eyes are more,
and more or less green, I'd say, a rust-
flecked moss, perhaps. The lyrical vulture
flexes his wings a little, on the ground
with her, you and no drama: and I wait.
There are wharves outside and landing stages built
liquid on rippling night, and there are stars
pendulous and luscious. You can push
her waking carcase out across a ledge
and sit with her in the reviving dark
against a plank that shines out its
broken oysters, weedy limpnesses.

It would be nice to hear from me on the
matter of trust, but no, just do
what you like to the oyster-woman, but
note that 'to' not 'with', and save some fear
for later. Now, where were we: on
the ground. And the woman woken well
and she discerns you in the stars,
and your hands from the jagged shells, and your tones
in the mosses' salt whisper, a sigh
that belongs to the water and slips back down
fathoms down before the light can come.
You owe me this: the way she breaks apart
and the enclasping spectrum curves its gloss
on you as you lie open at her heart. And what
salt meat will I require and who will ask
or bargain that I might provide us less,
for what is a joined journey from the start.
I will not answer, would not waste your time.
You are already with me and have brought
no company except my promises.

part two

What company except my promises
could keep you now in all your following
when all that seems to offer is that shape
spreadeagled like a spider in his blood
when all you feel on your hands congeals
into a vicious sweetness, cloying like
raw sugar on the lining of the veins.
You feel his death within you as it spins.
Your nerve-tips are the finest threads from it.
You see: the woman done, this is the man.
He's not more dead than she was. He's
alive and you are quite free to explore. Yes,
ignore that first ignoble moral
scruple. And, yes, I think your hands
should at first touch his face
before they stiffen to unlock the tie
and fidget with the shirt's top button and

delve in the blood on the jacket.
You see now. You trust me. We weren't
either now shocked by the kiss. I'm glad
you did kiss the subject: he could
have guessed it in there, somewhere.
Why not the eyelids? Yes. You can.
and easily undress the rest of him.
It worries you that the small
penis stirs in its slumber, but
that's because of memories, this
is one dying thing that can
not visibly piss blood. Or swell
out like a vegetable that screams,
and pin you to his dreams. You can
disengage and still provoke a prize.
I watch and I am learning
what you like. It was the flinch
of some ungoverned muscle in his side
beneath your thumbtip that convinced you
most about yourself. You smiled,
and your mouth kissed famous blood.
And antelopes breathe in the garden.
Their oxygen flows, but is still,
the milkiest of ways, and their limbs
tense with lovely fright. Tonight.
Tonight the shadows twitch suspiciously,
impenetrably deathly in the trees.
We won't, for we are calm. And we
won't speak of the rose-crystal, over which
a primary kind of pristine water flows.
Just turn him now and take him, blood
will lubricate all conquests, and this park
has fences keeping all the vandals out. No
one but I can see, and you have come
here, and here is nothing you can mourn. It
isn't to the gates that I escort you, but
it isn't to escape that you have come.

part three

It isn't to escape that you have come.
Triangles mirage on sky's night like
a migraine and the steel morning snips
first knifetips along treetops and is cold,
as cold as you are designate to be.
The dagger you are designate to be
has cut the haunches of an antelope
recognisably into food. It clinks
to help you convey pieces to your tongue.
The park's unkempt with pieces of the tongue.
Groomed dogs howl at the spikes for that.
Their hunger bends the fence-bars over them.
If it were to escape that you had come
this place has holes enough to shield it.
The woman and the man are dead and lie.
The woman and the man have gone and come.
You never were the woman and the man.
You never were the antelope, to flinch
into the plaited haywire of the rope
and follow it on tidy, drunken hooves
to here - so far and practical -
where the altar is an anvil and
the victim trussed and suitable
for a carboot or a ritual, as
we choose. Or a triangle, here.
It joins you to our journey from the start
and you, still lonely with my promises,
provide this communion that is not
an entree but an entrance, nourishment
on famous anguish, bloodlessly pristine
except if frozen crystals rouge your arms
to melt and lubricate a victory
which I have planned for you. The
roping water flinches on your own
throat in such hope and frailty
you understand the hind and how its limbs
shudder and enlock. No
one but I am watching, wait, no one

walks the black salt wharf where the
rose-crystal sets an opened woman hard
in her own light, the slithering moon-
colours of the oyster. You can go
down there and you can watch her through the gate
and leave the upturned man amongst the leaves.
No piss or blood or fantasies. He is
superfluous in conquest. Parchment haloes
crumble like april, dry their veins
where his fingers splay the ground. Their veins
now dry as if snapped from their branches.
It isn't by the gates that you arrive
but you are designated for reward.
If all things here were penetrably live,
you would trust in an escape by promises.
It would be to escape that I have come.

part four

It isn't to escape that I have come, but
your other's body's thin enough to hold,
is artefactually fragile. Its ribs
are milk in jade, and cyclamen
now dregs its locks like burgundy.
A statuesque resistance fills its kiss,
and every pulse is subtle, is a watch
to tell me time and date and where and this,
exclusive as a dream.
My feet are crisped to gold from travelling.
My hands are hot, as aired blood sways to them.
I gulp the pyre's smoke. Nothing bought's
so addictive or expensive, or
will taste of what I met,
except this air. Oh, here
exclaims against itself, accused,
and lacquers your drenched hair in tragedy,
Oh here, and now, oh why, as if
the meat you met was not already salt, or
blood was never pointed at its heart. Now
nothing sprawls forward, except I

in the open knees of the sun.
My limbs move me along more, so
my sweat can give me shade.
It isn't to escape now that you go,
it isn't recreation of a time
or a novelty which trees provide,
bare black in calculus across
one moon.
The park won't fence its equals out,
the notorious water or woodsmoke.
How could a hooded altar shine
but civil as a shambles? Could
the antlers and small hooves be true
unless to sing through ivory gaps
anonymous from every bend ahead,
sing circles apt as promises,
sing mine?
You are alright now, and must come.
It's alright. You pocket evidence less
fumid than sweetbreads on branches,
and quieter than carbon in
embedded fossils, monoxide rooms,
lungs in a slum autopsy. Hate
slums gingerly in the park tonight.
My face is too rigid for it.
Yes, I will kneel down and wait
for this ornament to overflow its ash
and give you your thin mattress
in fat ground. If it was
to sleep in this subject that you stumbled,
it was to escape you that it came.
Escorted here with nothing but its promise,
it trusted me to trust it to your gate.

part five

You trusted me to trust them to your gate
and here they are! Your friends and mine,
this lady and this gentleman, their pet.
Three lessons in good manners to us all,

since manners are resurrection.
It is to resurrect you they have come.
and no, I watch. With the quenching dusk
I pavilion and furnish the park
and tread the cinders under grassy silk.
I will escort them in, and bow.
The coatracks are many and empty,
except to support legends, silverly.
The woman converts simply to a chair.
The man becomes a table, well. The small
antelope sits feeding now.
It is clovenly exquisite,
picking softly at smoked entrails
with its enormous dagger.
See the woodwhorls shine like hair.
You will smile and remember
how her hair polished your mouth
red to red, to red. Too red,
light flinches from the chair to touch
electrically the tabletop,
on which your fingers stutter.
Be more polite. Sit down!
I see, you do. You see she is all silken
under you. His edge
confines your scissored flank with
tender pressure. Come. You can
be touched quite freely again.
Your tears are not ridiculed by water.
The water here is white with bowls
and fountains. I have only
come to empty ashtrays, to clean
cages. Take your meal. Take
the golden-white oysters, blond wines.
All the pups at the spikes are fed.
We will not worry. The blood
out there enlimits only
flat silhouettes in green.
Scrape in your chair more.
The little creature blushes,

licks its hoof. All etiquette
will forget some or other promises.
But here all are superlatively safe.
Safe here, and there never was another,
if it were to escape it that we came.
Ah, yes, and yes, you really should take ease
strip down to your shirtsleeves at last
and pour your red hair, flood the glass
and we will drink to you –
who'll never now be stranger to
our gates, which you must soon accept are gone.

ELAINE GOLDING

Genesis/take 2

lying beneath the tree
she's heady with the perfection
of moist ripe flesh
caught between exploring fingers
marvels at shape and texture
takes quiet pleasure
in sticky sweet juices
creeping beneath unpolished fingernails
decides to keep a secret –
but he approaches
envious of the new found playmate
afraid of any contest
between it
and his own voluptuous substance
thus, reluctantly she reveals the fruit
lying softly between her legs
presses it to his mouth –

and knows there'll be trouble in Paradise tonight.

AILEEN CORPUS

blkfern-jungal

wlk'n down regent street i see
blks hoo display blknez
(i min they sens of blknez)
n they say t' me . . .

        'ime gonna lif yoo outta
        yor blk hole n sho yoo
        how t' wlk n dress n tlk.'

n i sit in th' gutta
of regent street
(outside wair we ol meet)
n i look up n see
arown th'haylo of they hair,
a cosmetic afro ring –
a shiny haze
like it blines me man!!

so mu eyes go down t' thair
smart soot ol prest n cleen,
n'thair hi heel kork shooz
n i turn mu head n look at mu
soiled blknez, n i sezs . . .

        'ime gonna lif yoo outta
        yore blk hole n sho yoo
        how t' walk n dress n tlk.'

Taxi Conversation

i never had a woman like you.
what woman do you mean?
you know.
no.
i mean a black woman.
oh.
they say they're better than white.
who? do we say, or men who've seen the light?
other men, white men black men, what do you say?
i don't know driver, you see i've never had
a woman black or white.

i take a drag
exhale
my words are gone.
here it comes, he's gonna ask
about my men.

have you tried white men?
why?
how do they compare?
compare with whom?
with black men or do you only black?

the silence drones
the cars race
honking out a pace
the cab stops
the meter clicks
he turns to take my fare
but there i am no more.

why should i pay and submit
to cabbage minds like that
when i smell i can tell
a violent racist bait?

JEAN KENT

To the Ironingboard

It's not supposed to be like this:
illicit bliss taking you in my arms.
By all sociological decrees we're incompatible.

And yet we meet again.
You in your faded cotton slip
no longer the colour of marigolds, your old foam padding
edging out like moss after last week's damp.
So constant, unhumanly uncomplaining – only twice
in ten years have you refused to hold my iron
devotedly, like a hot red rose between your teeth;
only twice have you casually unwrenched your mouth
your teeth chattering silver uproarious onto the tiles
while you, neat as a secretary crossing her knees
tried out the game of passive resistance.

I know you had other plans. Once.
You wanted to be a ballerina but
your feet were too big. Your arms however
are eloquently expansive. They make a flat earth
where the geography of thought is unconfined. At your altar
of heat you steam out my wrinkles you make my mind
spit – you ought to be embarrassed
by that soft hiss of dreams.

But you stand here acceptant as earth,
your feet in a ready position. You could be hearing
music, or discord, of your own.   Tell me,
before you were bolted rigid did you learn more
than this one dance, this going down to the floor flatter
than any melancholy day I've ever known? Did you steal
a pinup of Nureyev or Margot Fonteyn? Is that the true strength
of your mettle?   Oh *you*,
with your stiff flamingo knees,
contrary as Alice redreaming Wonderland

I tuck you under my arm. Wearied, half-waking
I cut you like a pack of cards. Shuffle you back
to the wall. Doom you, like the factory workers
who made you, to repeat your one sad skill.

When all the world is finally blazed flat I suspect
this is how you'll be. Amid the ashes,
a burn on the mind.
Still beaming: *Watch me! Watch me   do the splits*

ANIA WALWICZ

Daredevil

I tried this play one day. My father leaves his medicines open. I take a
random bottle. I swig. I'm done for. Walk around so proud to have done
something big. I'm John Dare. I'm a devil. I'm Evel Knievel that jumped
over twenty buses. On his motorcycle. I'm not scared. Life's good and sharp.
Here for the last time I'm not bored. I'm seven and I've read every book
in the world. I know everything. I'm an electric girl. World's my oyster.
I'm its pearl.

Little Red Riding Hood

I always had such a good time, good time, good time girl. Each and every
day from morning to night. Each and every twenty-four hours I wanted
to wake up, wake up. I was so lively, so livewire tense, such a highly pitched
little. I was red, so red so red. I was a tomato. I was on the lookout for
the wolf. Want some sweeties, mister? I bought a red dress myself. I bought
the wolf. Want some sweeties, mister? I bought a red dress for myself.
I bought a hood for myself. Get me a hood. I bought a knife.

Leaving

In a week I won't be here any more. We are leaving and going away.
Goodbye everybody. I've got a new coat to travel in. Blue with fur. I don't
go to school any more. I don't care. I go to pictures every day. I'm already
gone from here. I can't imagine other people in my house. We are leaving
everything. Like it is. Beds unmade and the bedding. The ship came early
too early. So we're going. They had a warrant for my father's arrest. So
we have to go. I wanted to travel. I was born inside the house I'm leaving
behind. Floors floors dark rooms built by the photographer and the cellar.
Goodbye to the attic and I said goodbye to the sea goodbye that summer.
We are going away. Maybe jungle different land and happy. Scared to
leave I get this fear of the road. I had a bad dream one night. I don't want

to think about it. It isn't my idea. We're going to go away. He built a big wooden box to put things in. Some things. Not much. Wrapped the painting. The house so strange in winter with clothes on a string inside the room. This is in the middle already. We are not there and we are no longer here. I go to the cinema. I'm not anywhere. Nowhere. On the cinema screen. You can laugh. We laugh and we are packing. And the house messy. The box man jokes. Are you trying to strangle me with these ropes for clothes. We laugh. And we leave. And everything's in between places. Hanging.

Marcel Proust

Marcel Proust eats the cake and his childhood comes back to him. One night I met him in a pub. Big hazel eyes. Tall and dark. Asked if he could talk. Lived in Toorak Road. Didn't work. All day long, he slept. Then, at night, he shaved and it happened. Cut himself. With his blade. By accident. And his childhood came back to him. Just like that. All at once, he was a little boy. German. That lost the war. His mother didn't love him. She beat him. I'm Marcel Proust. I'm this dark handsome German. I sleep all day. All day long I sleep. All day long, all night long I sleep. At night I get up. I need a shave. I shave. I cut myself. Just one little cut. It bleeds. And my childhood comes back to me. I'm a little boy in Germany. My mother doesn't love me. My mother doesn't want me. She hits. I'm only a little boy again. With hazel eyes and dark hair. I'm German. My mother doesn't love me. I cut myself. My mother doesn't want me in Germany. That lost the war. I cut myself and I'm a little boy again. In Germany. I'm a little cut boy again in Germany. I'm a cut little boy in Germany. My mother beats me. I'm a hurt little boy in Germany. I lost the war. I cut myself, and my childhood comes back to me. Just one night, I cut myself and it does. Just like that. Suddenly.

Australia

You big ugly. You too empty. You desert with your nothing nothing nothing. You scorched suntanned. Old too quickly. Acres of suburbs watching the telly. You bore me. Freckle silly children. You nothing much.

With your big sea. Beach beach beach. I've seen enough already. You dumb dirty city with bar stools. You're ugly. You silly shoppingtown. You copy. You too far everywhere. You laugh at me. When I came this woman gave me a box of biscuits. You try to be friendly but you're not very friendly. You never ask me to your house. You insult me. You don't know how to be with me. Road road tree tree. I came from crowded and many. I came from rich. You have nothing to offer. You're poor and spread thin. You big. So what. I'm small. It's what's in. You silent on Sunday. Nobody on your streets. You dead at night. You go to sleep too early. You don't excite me. You scare me with your hopeless. Asleep when you walk. Too hot to think. You big awful. You don't match me. You burnt out. You too big sky. You make me a dot in the nowhere. You laugh with your big healthy. You want everyone to be the same. You're dumb. You do like anybody else. You engaged Doreen. You big cow. You average average. Cold day at school playing around at lunchtime. Running around for nothing. You never accept me. For your own. You always ask me where I'm from. You always ask me. You tell me I look strange. Different. You don't adopt me. You laugh at the way I speak. You think you're better than me. You don't like me. You don't have any interest in another country. Idiot centre of your own self. You think the rest of the world walks around without shoes or electric light. You don't go anywhere. You stay at home. You like one another. You go crazy on Saturday night. You get drunk. You don't like me and you don't like women. You put your arm around men in bars. You're rough. I can't speak to you. You burly burly. You're just silly to me. You big man. Poor with all your money. You ugly furniture. You ugly house. Relaxed in your summer stupor. All year. Never fully awake. Dull at school. Wait for other people to tell you what to do. Follow the leader. Can't imagine. Work horse. Thick legs. You go to work in the morning. You shiver on a tram.

modern ballroom dancing

victor sylvester says. social habits poise grace pleasure rhythm. learn to dance. style balance no prancing on tip toe. up to date. use your body. let your legs swing easy. no freaks. elementary figures last you a lifetime. ballroom orchestra tempo. gentlemans hold. stand erect head poised grasp lady hold her directly steer and control lady with his body. lady is poised.

lady never attempts to lead or guide her partner. submit yourself entirely
to him. do not lean on him or anticipate what next. just follow. gentleman
raise hand to partners palm downwards close fingers. don't taut don't hunch
don't hold your breath. flat foot toes first. never out of time. stride skim
glide don't ape. look as though you are enjoying it. if you want to talk
sit out. lady don't push your foot out you will tread on your partners toes.
here's a little suggestion for gentlemen when dancing think of yourself as
trying gently to push your partner over. keep that idea at the back of your
mind. full stride weight heel back ball on your toes use your ankle move
forward pulling partner hip break at waist turn shoulders only trunk body
in one piece pulling muscles tango sway towards walls. steering rests with
the man his duty to follow course difficult if lady tall get someone small.
move as one person. looks perfect couples beautiful to watch. lean forward
hips. fall away. learn to walk backwards ladies. beat beats beat slow quick
waltz rumba samba contrary promenade. fall away turn do the figure you
intended to do join one to another. slow foxtrot develop from chase. smarter
ballrooms. sway feather raise and fall. gentleman impetus turn. lady step
to side. gentleman complete figure. lady hover. gentleman cross. lady step
back. natural twist. gentleman step forward. pull lady back. gentleman
step through. lady walk around partner. gentleman step forward. lady
step backwards. gentleman forward. lady no foot rise. wing telemark top
spin swivel. gentleman cross. lady swivelling. gentleman forward. lady
contrary body movement. box natural turn. gentleman turn. lady finish
with back to wall. closed change reverse turn natural spin double reverse
spin impetus turn whisk drag backward. while gentleman does his steps
forward. lady does hers backward. quick step swivel pivot. gentleman
reverse turn. lady follows. lady step back. while gentleman does three steps
lady makes four. gentleman en face. lady back to drag body. he turn lady.
cross swivel fish tail. gentleman in front of lady. he starts to run away.
tango man holds her on his side. lock your thighs. unlock your thighs.
gentleman step. lady step back. gentleman forward. lady step back. rumba.
gentleman cross. lady on side. latin rhythm samba joy dance. pulsating
gaiety. gentleman knee action weight. lady turn back to wall. corta jack.
gentleman forward. lady back. samba. gentleman whisks lady. botofago.
gentleman face. lady repeats. samba. gentleman relax. lady turns. waltz.
man heel pivot comfortable. lady hesitation balance. gentleman spins lady.

JENNY BOULT

admiring the handiwork

it's just the right size
i knew it would be now turn round
while i adjust the shoulders

you're not standing up straight
that's better   you can't see
this particularly lovely piece
right in the middle of your back
but it's very good

& there's a great colour combination
just under the right arm   move
over here a bit   the sleeve
is a bit twisted   that's better

turn round now   slowly   you'd
never make a model   no dear
that's not fair   of course you aren't
just a coathanger

i love you very much   but
i need to have a proper look at it
there's a loose thread there
don't move   these scissors are very sharp

of course you'll still be around
to wear it   how else could i admire
my handiwork   don't frown   it's
exactly the right size   fold the cuffs
up a bit   that's better   now
you can look in the mirror   smile dear
it's beautiful

scene

Behind the counter, the kettle is boiling,
the cups are in the sink demanding a wash
and all i can do is stare outside watching
everyone go by thinking . . . it's a great day

The old men at the tables are having an
argument; the other table is not
concerned
Yanni has decided to take a nap behind
the cigarette machine;
in the far end of the partition the little
Albanian is resting his eyes

On the pool table the Yugoslavs are sitting
drinking their cokes, eyeing the waitress
the young Australians are playing the
flipper machine,
outside near the toilets the Rod Stewarts
have set fire to the cardboard boxes

Tension builds, the noise gets louder
and louder,
i stay put behind the counter, the Bosses
aint in.

WENDY JENKINS

Against Noise
(After a poetry reading)

To let words be time
and tick that way
    now
        now
gaps like doors that let you in
to lie down on the furniture,
much of which, you find,
is like your own.

Things left for you by the host:
Snapshots, mirrors, a bowl of blood,
the taste of which is slightly sour,
lovely birds and poignant flowers,
knives away in drawers
or on the table.

(Oustide a rooster crows
and a horse *is* white
in metaphorical rain.)

Against noise,
for time,
to find a way
into a said geography,
to hear that slow and special clock
    now
            now
In the spaces there
pick up the knife.
Try your thumb along that blade.

CHRIS MANSELL

Definition Poem: Pissed as a Parrot

For those of you who are etymologically inclined
I would like to take this opportunity
to explain to you the derivation of the expression
pissed as a parrot.

Sidney Baker in *The Australian Language* indexes
        Paroo dog
        Parrot
        Parson's pox
There is no entry under *pissed.*
he also gives
        Proverbial, come the
        Piss, panther's
and   Pseudoxy.

Parrot on page 55 is a sheep
which has lost some of its wool.
If the sheep's fly-blown it's a rosella.

Wilkes in his *Dictionary of Australian Colloquialisms*
lists only to piss in someone's pocket
(refer Kylie Tennant, Bray, Hardy & Herbert)
Pissant around (Dymphna Cusack)
and Pissant, game as a.
There is no mention of any parrot in any condition at all.

In *Collins English Dictionary* (Australian edition)
you will find definitions for
        piss
        piss about
        Pissaro
        piss artist
and   piss off.

Parrots appear in their psittaciformes capacity
which I found meant having a short hooked bill,
to mimic.
It was not entirely clear whether this referred to birds.

Parrot-fashion had nothing to do with anything.

Roget's *Thesaurus*
Nuttal's *Dictionary of Synonyms and Antonyms*
Stillman's *Poets Manual and Rhyming Dictionary*
Webster's *Treasury of Synonyms, Antonyms and Homonyms*
and the *Shorter Oxford English Dictionary*
were no help at all.

I thought *Usage & Abusage*
being by Partridge
could be illuminating, but it appears
that neither piss nor parrots are abused.

I refused to consult Strunk's *Elements of Style*
on the grounds that the backcover blurb
has quotes from the *Greensboro Daily News*
and *The Telephone Engineers and Management Journal*.

But I went to afternoon tea
in the School of Chemistry at the University of Sydney
at 4 pm on Thursday 6 November
and there, Dr A. R. Lacey, physical chemist, MSc PhD,
informed me, in his capacity as a true blue,
down to earth, dinky-di, grass roots Aussie that
when working on his horse stud in the Wingecarribee Shire
he had observed that Gang Gang cockatoos
fall with paralytic suddenness
from the branches of Hawthorn bushes
after ingesting the berries.

Incredibly, *The Reader's Digest Complete Book of Australian Birds*
makes no mention of this.

Lady Gedanke Writes to the Painter

I am ignorant about art
it makes me wordless
tongueless unable to swallow
anything I always look
at the frames instead
because the edge
is obvious and I avoid
your studio because of all
the unframed things I cannot
understand how you do not eat
the cadmium yellow
or phthalo blue
or why you don't prime
your face brilliant white
I have never
understood red and black
seems too theoretical
so what this portrait is
I have no idea though
the frame has one or both of us
enclosed there is me
but then perhaps
we look like one another
you are the one with the frame
catching things to paste down
with twigs of colour
I am the one illustrating
a fear of edges
punching out black
absences from white pages

the painter is Jenni Mitchell — *eds.*

Dialogue

there's her camel gait down the hall she pretends
she's a dancer there's a machine gun for a laugh
I know I understand people do it all the time
look at me pretending to write but scared
of words I know I understand

read about religion want a needle or a psychiatrist or
priest or politician or money or a friend or a father
to fix it all up I know I understand people do it
all the time someone on the radio talking about poetry
(god help us)

as if you or I gave a stuff about it people do
it all the time and it's not fair that his lover did
what she did people do it all the time and there's others
picking the balls of unidentifiable something
off their cardigans

like fat girls always getting in the bad word first
before someone else gets it in you shrug your pain
around you like indifference people do it all the time
I know I understand I shoulder my indifference
like it was pain

people do it all the time she points out the landscape
in case someone looks at her she tells me her lover
is impotent I know he goes out to find a bigger
motorbike complains about toilet paper hair pins knives
people do it all the time I understand

DOROTHY PORTER

from The Nashville Poems

Jealousy drove the bus
    and parked the car.
Oh, what a ride!
And I awoke and found me here
on the cold hill's side.

It's even further to Brisbane
    with summer heat
taking the mickey
    out of
        loving talk –
and that's why
    I'm happier in winter
when ice-cream wrappers
        are withered from the beach
and no blondes sing.

How happy are you
    with off-peak television?
Too little sleep
too much coffee
wake up
    strangling in your hair
        diagnosed
La Talk Back Radio
    hath thee in thrall!

Call it poverty then
call it yer soul
    playing its greatest hits
call it
    thinking of your terrific lover
making sweet moan
    elsewhere tonight.

The Red Sports Car Afternoon

In this kind
of weather,
that reminds me
far too much
of apple blossom
and holidays in
the mountains
as a kid,
I am without garters
without rules –

even a laundromat
in the freezing cold
can be romantic
when a new place
is just a movie,
you don't mind pestering
the locals
or talking too loudly
imagining yerself
in a turtle neck sweater
narrow eyed
in black n' white.

Then a blond
in a red sports car
falls for you
and you for him
because in 16 millimetre
you can't lose –

he says he's married
nonchalantly
before you start kissing
but to yourself
you're even more two dimensional
than his wife
so you snatch at
his mouth, hands
and armfuls of
bizarre affection
and stand under trees
under lights
on the beach
and think up
incoherent lines neat.

Wow.
We say together.
How did this happen
and Are you all right
I feel confused
We'll think it over
tonight –

me sleeping
in the bower-bird's
nest
of a stranger's blue books
you with yer wife.

C'est la vie.
I must have said.
It's aspros with coke

for when the
        house-lights
go up
    hissing
like an all night train sludge
    of relatives
        and morality.

One way
    or another
I'm gonna find ya
I'm gonna getcha
            getcha –

the beauty of rock music
its sexual
    optimism
every collection
    collects groupies
    collects dust
    collects people on
        holiday
where every second
    is a silver plane
and showing off
    to the hosties
I'm from Sydney Megalopolis!
    and I work
    for 'The Daily Planet'
and all I want
    is a married man –

I will give you
    my finest hour
the one I spent
    watching you shower
his wife singing
    in the carburettor
of a red sports car –

freezing cold weather
our commercial
    has goose-bumps
this movie
    is kero-
blue and fantastic

a line I've used
    in another poem
about snow
about happiness
about an 'Alpine' ad
now
        blue n' fantastic
I smell kero
I can see me
    setting you
        on fire
and it working too –

I mean a wedding
    celebrant
quoting Desiderata
    in a heat wave –

and *now*
    it's a red sports car
        roaring
like the inside of a pistol
and a poetry reading
    when a blond
followed me
    home like a
        fall of glittering snow
in a Russel Drysdale
    Xmas card
        and drove me off
in a red sports car that was
    double-jointed.

Scenes From A Marriage

from The Night Parrot

V

Nothing so sweet
nothing so obscene
*   as my lover and me*
*   will ever be*
*   shown on TV*

this fragment,
    from a pop song I imagined,
        stuck in my throat
            helplessly
    during the coldest night
    of the year
when mixed passionate breath
            fogged up
                every window
                every mirror
                every TV set
                    in my house
while I collapsed cosy, trivial
            and tender –

then in coffee's camaraderie
        a silt
    like Lake Eyre parched white
when the night parrot
        questioned my fidelity
when the night parrot
        arrived home.

Tristesse –
        and watching through smudged glass
the wind
        savaging a sapling –

this trapped tyranny
        of watching
                nothing

and conjuring violence
    from the magic powder
        of boredom, –

I'm a deserted wife
    listlessly watching
        tomato soup
    as if it were 'Gone with the Wind' –

it's the dry season
    the night parrot
        is starving
    and won't mate
        can't nest
    and finds my water
        bitter,
we're fighting
    and I say
        like a whining suburb
        sculpted by salt bush
            and Campbelltown land developers
            this is your desert, not mine!

Trial Separation

from The Night Parrot

I

In high summer
   heat-stroke
     grabs me by the heels
and throws me
     into a dry creek bed
where the night parrot
       clucks in the cracks –

I'm parched, giddy, afraid
   imploring water
     from the wrong man –

I'm in drought!
   I complain
     to the deaf night parrot –

I trusted the river
   and followed it numbly
until it disappeared
       very suddenly
         into grey mud –
in my despair
     like phantom ringing in the head
I kept hearing
   a waterfall
     roaring
       around the next bend.

ANNE LLOYD

Juds park

The tin shed housed
only scorers and lazy spectators;
flies hovering, the last legs of lunch.
Girls waddled out, their not too white
armour dangling on sunburnt thighs.
Most dared it barefoot, simply trusting.
Between mine, the nursed can cold
of droplets trickling down shins dust
feet, face hoping you wouldn't see
me seeing you, a guzzling of beer.

They made me stand by a can though,
marker, head and shoulders
foolishly covered with someone else's
sombrero. Outfielding, and missing the ball
to please, but pleased you could not see me
be seeing you even before that rubbing of
ball on creams the sharp click spikes tearing
out remaining grass. Down. Thunder. It was
twenty years I never and then the slow body arc,
the whisk of a dragon-fly flick in the sun,
coupled, mated, fast, she's out.

GIG RYAN

If I Had a Gun

I'd shoot the man who pulled up slowly in his hot car this
                                        morning
I'd shoot the man who whistled from his balcony
I'd shoot the man with things dangling over his creepy chest
in the park when I was contemplating the universe
I'd shoot the man who can't look me in the eye
who stares at my boobs when we're talking
who rips me off in the milk-bar and smiles his wet purple smile
who comments on my clothes. I'm not a fucking painting
that needs to be told what it looks like.
who tells me where to put my hands, who wrenches me into
                                        position
like a meccano-set, who drags you round like a war
I'd shoot the man who couldn't live without me
I'd shoot the man who thinks it's his turn to be pretty
flashing his skin passively like something I've got
to step into, the man who says *John's a chemistry Phd*
and an ace cricketer, Jane's got rotten legs
who thinks I'm wearing perfume for him
who says *Baby you can really drive* like it's so complicated,
male, his fucking highway, who says *ah but you're like that*
and pats you on the head, who kisses you at the party because
everybody does it, who shoves it up like a nail
I'd shoot the man who can't look after himself
who comes to me for wisdom
who's witty with his mates about heavy things
that wouldn't interest you, who keeps a little time
to be human and tells me, female, his ridiculous
private thoughts. Who sits up in his moderate bed
and says *Was that good* like a menu
who hangs onto you sloppy and thick as a carpet
I'd shoot the man last night who said *Smile honey*
don't look so glum with money swearing from his jacket
and a 3-course meal he prods lazily

who tells me his problems: his girlfriend, his mother,
his wife, his daughter, his sister, his lover
because women will listen to that sort of rubbish
Women are full of compassion and have soft soggy hearts
you can throw up in and no-one'll notice
and they won't complain. I'd shoot the man
who thinks he can look like an excavation-site
but you can't, who thinks what you look like's for him
to appraise, to sit back, to talk his intelligent way.
I've got eyes in my fucking head. Who thinks if he's smart
he'll get it in. I'd shoot the man who said
Andrew's dedicated and works hard, Julia's ruthlessly ambitious
who says *I'll introduce you to the ones who know*
with their inert alcoholic eyes
that'll get by, sad, savage, and civilised
who say *you can* like there's a law against it
I'd shoot the man who goes stupid
in his puny abstract how-could-I-refuse-she-needed-me
taking her tatty head in his neutral arms like a pope
I'd shoot the man who pulled up at the lights
who rolled his face articulate as an asylum
and revved the engine, who says *you're paranoid*
with his educated born-to-it calm
who's standing there wasted as a rifle
and explains the world to me. I'd shoot the man who says
Relax honey come and kiss my valium-mouth blue.

Not Like a Wife

He questions her, his face soft with lovely money.
Be my mistress. He's French, polite as corruption.
Yes. Her clothes are dirty. Love has made me poor.
She leans against the flimsy cupboard, wrapping her face up
in her hands. I loved a rich man
once, but I was never blonde, and suntans you know,
so bland. I never looked American enough
on the beach.

I'll take you to Bangkok he says, the jewellery.
I can't wear it. The nightclubs. Yes.
You could look like a million dollars you know,
touching her shirt collar, if you had it.
I can't cook. His dark eyes soft and persistent
as flesh, wise with money he talks.
You like it here yes, you find character in poverty?
His arms snatch the whole creaking house up.
He's laughing at the plaster. You're so frank and evasive.
It's alright, really, tense as a movie,
watching carlights flash above the bed.
He loved me once. You're new, aren't you.

The sink's blocked in Darlinghurst.
I never could eat spaghetti effectively,
too unmarried or something.

Cruising

I dreamt I drank too much lemonade
and it was fatal. Everybody pointed and ran.
The man came into my room in his office clothes.
Go away I said, and I jumped out of my skin.

In the Italian cafe, I think of the wealthy.
What helicopter must have sunk into the roof
to be used so precariously by the management,
or contrived. (It's common *now*)
I stare at the propeller, it shudders like a failure.
Who can eat under that?

You can see from the street they've added another story.
The pilot's capsule's been renovated, hired out
for secret occasions, furtive and giddy, so secret
we never heard. I'd find it claustrophobic
and ruin my clothes. (After the bill gets drenched,
the waiter takes it to dry in a microwave oven)
A friend told me it's been rigged without gravity,
looking red and expensive. His mouth sloped down,
about to reveal something xenophobic. I had to leave.

Is there a word which means 'fear of things falling on you'?
I wake up and look at the split in my ceiling.
I jumped out of my skin again, glad that I smoke,
glad that I can become historical and calm at the same time,
thinking of how non-smokers taste when you kiss them,
pink and wet and physical like a baby.

His Cubist Drawings

You're shivering in the Cross, this mad bar,
with him all dreaming and response.
By the time you get home, you've lost the urge,
but think of him, he infiltrates your head even,
his cold bike taking off and your free hand dream.

Fun is enforced in a moment. It will wipe
most of you out, as you bring him round gradually,
being used to it. Leave your brain on that chair
and let Feelings just kick-start out of nothing.
Ennui is what the rich feel.

. . . .

His cubist drawings are lying everywhere
between the dripping virgin and his male despair
that suffers, seeing nothing, in this neat artistic house.
Your sense of urgency would kill a car.

He borrows the mirror for hours to prove his clothes
are special. He shows you his delicate jewel.
You're supposed to sigh, and help him
with his coat, but talking about it makes me sick.
His pretty face swooning in the door is interruptive, male,
and the question, curious, oppressive. You will cut
that shiny ribbon to get out.

A woman I love falls out of a strange shop
in the middle of nowhere. I want to be better.
Her fast mouth and her hand.
I'm about to have breakfast at 3 p.m.
on his money. I feel like a mess.
Her thin head turning and buried
is a good way to be.

JUDITH BEVERIDGE

The Domesticity of Giraffes

She langorously swings her tongue
like a black leather strap as she chews
and endlessly licks the wire for salt
blown in from the harbour.
Bruised-apple eyed she ruminates
towards the tall buildings
she mistakes for a herd:
her gaze has the loneliness of smoke.

I think of her graceful on her plain –
one long-legged mile after another.
I see her head framed in a leafy bonnet
or balloon-bobbing in trees.
Her hide's a paved garden of orange
against wild bush. In the distance, running,
she could be a big slim bird just before flight.

Here, a wire-cripple –
legs stark as telegraph poles
miles from anywhere.
She circles the pen, licks the wire,
mimics a gum-chewing audience
in the stained underwear of her hide.
This shy Miss Marigold rolls out her tongue

like the neck of a dying bird.
I offer her the fresh salt of my hand
and her tongue rolls over it
in sensual agony, as it must
over the wire, hour after bitter hour.
Now, the bull indolently
lets down his penis like a pink gladiolus
drenching the concrete.

She thrusts her tongue under his rich stream
to get moisture for her thousandth chew.

Making Perfume

So, that summer I picked everything:
the hibiscus that shut at six o'clock,
the white-pollened flower
I called The Baker's Daughter,
the yellow rose that lasted weeks beyond its season
and the great pale flower with a cold look –
Queen in the Tower.

Then I took some bottles from their cupboards
and their lids twirled off and their perfume
came three voices high in my head.
I lined them like wineglasses on the sill
and filled each with petals and water
and gave them keyboard names like
Chandelier and Tier on Golden Tier.

I remember how I lived that summer
in a room with a thousand windows in blue and green.
I'd stay out late to pick and soak the petals
and pour them into bottles and bury them in the earth
with a made-up name for a simple flower plus water.
Later, I'd wash and line the bottles on the sill
and read their labels until each one rang

a terrace of bells in my head.
I mourned the bottles I named for my heroines of hopeless love
and stood them in kitchentapwater
and stored them out of the light.
I dreamt of Balls, dinner roses,
a woman gently naming herself to herself.

Now, I wonder whatever happened to Lavinia,
the Fourteen Nights, Ballet Blanc,
the fragrance in the blue twirled bottle
I named Pirouette.
Months later I probably poured them down the sink.

But no-one suspected that summer
why my eyes were suddenly circled with a dark pencil,

why my cheeks had the faint glow of day,
why I swished my skirts as I moved.

I kept the bottles with me, moved them about the room,
vowed not to open them for seven years
and named them after the girl kept at home
who never stopped saying as she stirred her pots:
'O, I wish, I wish, I wish . . .'

Streets of Chippendale

Streets named Ivy, Vine, Rose and Myrtle –
now lack a single tree. They could have been
the homes of kindly aunts in quiet suburbs
before factories like terrible relations

moved in, changed the place.
And Abercrombie (sounds like the eccentric,
unmarried third cousin) – you expect a place
where residents dressed in slacks and turtle necks

are walking pedigree dogs;
but Abercrombie's different –
hits the bottle with a dozen pubs,
grumbles like a drunk parent

to 'bloody well watch the road' as it crosses
to Hugo, Louis – they could be
respected gentlemen strolling past terraces
to call on the nearby Aunts:

but they're beer-mates of Abercrombie,
pub-crawlers that back on to Caroline in the dark,
where someone smashes the street-lights.
Sad daughter of the ruined slipper –

your body a mass of work-boot bruises.
Thomas and Edward have climbed

to renovated villas, leisure-hour balconies
trees, incomes. Abercrombie screeches cars,

questions their manhood, lands in trouble
with the police. Streets change character.
Suburbs go to the wall like families.
Ivy, Vine, Rose and Myrtle not one of your descendants

mourns your loss. Christian names mean nothing.
Your surname's dragged through police files –
strikes fear in pedestrians
who stray into one of its dark corners.

My Name

Someone is prowling around the borders of my name. They have
been there for days. I can't see them or hear them because in
the house of my name is a room of silence and a huge window of fog.
But I know they are there. My name is certified in a gold frame
that hangs on the room's wall. Everytime they move, it shakes.

At first I didn't worry. But now they have begun rubbing
their sleeve over my name's glass. They are rubbing in circles that
are gradually widening. I scream that they can't do this and
repeatedly show them the gold frame. They take no notice. They keep
on rubbing. They rub until the fog disappears and their face becomes
visible.

Now, I am afraid for my name's safety. The frame is shaking
more rapidly though I have set up all conceivable defences. I have
padded my name's wall with photos of myself. I have entered my name
on lists. I have dispatched letters in all possible directions.

Nothing is working. They have broken through my name's door
and are wandering the secret passageways as if everything's already
familiar. Perhaps they are a lost relative? When I question them they
glare sharply as if to say 'who do you think you are?' I run to get
them the gold frame. I look for it on the wall but all that's hanging
there is this person's coat, dusty and torn.

When I return I find the locks on my name's door have been
changed and I can go neither in nor out. I cannot yell for help.

ANNE BREWSTER

Ghoul

His kind smile is pasted like a poster
his comfortable eyes arranged
like the meticulous three-piece suit
contriving intimacy. He hints
that he abhors respectability picking
his words like lice, sticky with boredom.
He's slick, he's just like all the rest,
so cool, he does this every day
and asks conspicuously who is that girl,
his hooks so thin they fail the bait.
He's the man who knows the world
and girls inside out, he can give you a taste
of the good life, the one you covet
through shop windows. He talks like a telephone,
hiring sex. His wife doesn't trust him
but he's an individual who doesn't
wash up. He advertises availability
like an empty lot, craving dereliction.
He probes the imagined flesh, a ghoul
at the sideshow of rictal clowns.

SARAH DAY

Greenhouse Tomatoes

Inside the vast humidicrib
measured shade and warmth
and windlessness temper
an abundantly naive tomato crop.

Lulled by the pump's electric beat
soporific forms hang,
meditative, musing in
suspended animation.

I stay,
calmed
in the bloodstream
of this moist metabolism.

Like some gargoyle
whose gross spume
lifts a lump into
the onlooker's throat,

outside
a gushing ballcock
checks with shocking force
five hundred frenzied thirsts.

ISABEL HARTMAN

Check Mate

It was still raining hard outside,
So they'd postponed their picnic till next weekend
and he'd set up a chess board and lit a fire,
and altogether it was quite homely.

It's true, isn't it, she said, somewhat smugly,
That the queen's the most powerful piece on the board,
And can move, free-spirited, wherever she wishes.
In a way, he replied, but the king's still *the* most important piece.

The pristine bishops continued with oblique movements
To wipe out their opposing congregations.

The king, she said, as she castled,
Thinking about her English childhood,
Just seems to plod along and be defended.
I think of him as calculating, and prudent, he said.

She considered trying for a stalemate to finish the game,
So she could sit by the fire and stroke the cat instead.

He thinks he's playing draughts, she thought,
Just taking whatever he can with no regard for strategy.
Fool, he was thinking. I've always beaten you at chess.
I've beaten you at every game.

That night she slept dreaming of carefree chess pieces
And old English landscapes with sweet musty gardens,
While he, with his king piece, his most important piece,
Tried to penetrate her dreams.

But. Check.
He'd have to move. Or rearrange.
Or this time,
He'd lose.

AMANDA STEWART

romance

1st date 1st kiss 1st kiss 1st
fuck 1st/1st/1st/   relived
                 to be roses/candles/
moons/waves/beaches/idiosynchronize/
presents/chocolates/early   morning
lust/walks/fires/song/dance/hold   hands/
press close/meetin the eyes/hands/movement/hands/
move/lips/eyes/shoulder/nape/eyes/lobes/ears/eyes/
'till death us do part
                        ing is such sweet sor
                                          ry to s
                                               ay i
love y
      ou are the way the truth and the l
                                        ight of the
silvery moon rose is a rose is a rose is a way to s
                                                    ay i
love y
      ou are my love is love is love is love is love
is love

IT BECOMES: JULY 1981

IT'S OUTRAGE
US. I MEAN
WITH ALL THIS WITH ALL THIS I MEAN
IT'S ALL THIS.   O . IT'S
JUST DISGUSTING. IT'S IT'S IT'S
IT IS IT IS IT IS
OFF THE AIR/INCREDIBLE/OFF/HORRIFIC/TYPICAL/
I MEAN IT'S AMAZING IT'S
THATCHERFRAZERAEGUNRIGHTWINGWARWEDDINGREBELLION
POLICECAPAFEUDALIS.M.ACHOMONOPOLEADERS
WARNEWSCONTROLWARNEWSCONTROL.   I MEAN I MEAN
IT'S BECAUSE AND IT'S IT'S
I MEAN IT IS. I MEAN AND IT IS
IT IS IT IS IT IS IT IS IT IS IT IS
IT'S IT'S IT'S IT'S
IT. IT. IT.   IT   IT

KATE LILLEY

A Flash of Green

Dazed by summer at the washing line
I was hanging small wet bundles when you came.
The water ran dark furrows down
my breast where your face pressed hard, familiar.
Circling my cotton dress your arms
enclosed all possible weathers.

To love one man and then others, in the same way:
never to shake them off entirely.
I know my shape changes constantly
but I don't know what the changes are;
your face I can rearrange at will,
the malleable flesh of your untanned face.
In the noon heat by the washing line
I look at you again, more simply.
Your shadow slants back over the brick
and gorges itself on passionfruit vine:
you have its richness of colour and taste.

Since you first pointed out the sky
at any time of the day I stop
and put my bundles down and stare
at the lofty or sultry cloud formations –
how they lord it over the earth.

Fabula

1

Resurrecting my mother I fabricate
a narrative rich in detail.
In it we two are mapped layer on layer,
connections immanent in every choice.
Those stories not included I have
forgotten as insignificant
to me or my understanding of you.
The discontinuities are easiest to list:
daughter of a farm-girl I never went barefoot,
never rode a horse;
while you did correspondence and drew
pictures for the agricultural show
I pedalled to school on my bike,
ignoring the stop-signs.
When we drove to see 'the country'
I fell asleep in the back seat –
that was thirty years later, and I was your child.

2

Never saw your farm or even
a representation of it
but you once pulled out a photograph
of a farmhouse matched in style and period.
Although you had never been there you knew
the interior plan minutely.
Now I can describe it too using something
more than mimickry.
Our lives are not unique, discrete –
moments kidnapped from the general store
are hostages of need, instantial.
To catalogue myself I turn biographer
of a blood relation who is not dead,
relocating you in a fictive past
to which you have only partial access.
The course I chart holds good for now,
stands with earlier versions.

DIPTI SARAVANAMUTTU

Statistic for the New World

It's an ode to relationship
when you put your foot through
your Grandmother's bridal sheets.
I want to comfort you.
But you change personalities, as
pale blue mingles with the scar
on your shin while our bodies fit.
Heroic, I hold my cheek against
your neck, *I'm* not jealous.
I qualify your stance of
physical perfection like the Japanese
art of tattoo and we're worlds apart
if you lie about the ending.
You'll play a battered swan
and torture me until I'm stuck
on physical detail.
What have I learnt that's different?

LUCINDA CASTALDI

The Dummies

The sighting of the photograph has begun. The tourist stands behind
and slightly to the left of the three women. The women stand facing
the three dummies in the window. They are laughing. They are talking
in a story to themselves and to the dummies, for they are also
characters. The women are entranced by their story telling and cannot
leave the window.

All are caught by the square borders of the viewpoint finder. The
three women caught by the tourist. The tourist caught by his camera.
The dummies caught by fashion. The window between the women and
the dummies reflects all seven. One of the women places her hands on
the glass. In her story she would persuade the dummies to change
freely. She tells them of a place where people dress in clothes
that have no labels. The dummies are not impressed. They have an
affinity with the minds and the machines that made their clothes.
They scoff at her.

The wind is blowing the womens' clothes about them. The road
they stand in gives access only to pedestrians. The sun is setting
and reminds them of other days. The way autumn overlaps with spring
before meeting summer. They could in fact be somewhere else.
But they are not.

Another of the women leans close to the window. She giggles as she
places her lips on the glass. In her story the dummies are playing
with love. She explains how one of the dummies is desired by the
other two. And how this one likes to be wanted, but she is teasing
them. She is waiting to see which one desires her lips more. . The
dummies blush. One of them looks sharply at this woman. She practises
her perfect gaze. All together the dummies laugh in sharp
shrill notes. They are made to be desired by men, not women . . .

The tourist shifts position. He cannot quite get the women and the
dummies lined up together . . .

The last woman moves very close to the glass. She whispers her story
to the dummies. The dummies look as if they are paling, but it

might be the fading light. The other two women remember what this
story is about and in unison they touch their abdomens and sigh. The
woman telling the story makes it redder and throws in a groan
for good measure. The dummies refuse this story the most. Their body
size is precise, perfect, exact. They refuse any more even to listen.
The women all laugh with tears in their eyes. The dummies freeze their
eyes and close their minds.

The tourist sighs. There is almost no light left so he presses the
button. The polaroid makes whirring noises as the snap rolls out.
When he looks up from the finished dried photo the women are
gone. The dummies look the same.

CHARMAINE PAPERTALK-GREEN

Wanna be white

My man took off yesterday
with a waagin
He left me and the kids
To be something in this world
Said he was sick of being
black, poor and laughed at
Said he wanted to be white
have better clothes, a flash car
and eat fancy
He said me and the kids
would give him a bad name
because we are black too
So he left with a waagin

waagin — east coast word for 'white female',
        derived from 'white gin'.

ANNA MUNSTER

breaking the drought

in the summer in bed with the hot heat flies lying between
us. fucking and the sweat through the gauze sticks to this silence.
fucking and your breath shimmers in the red of an afternoon. i
could not force the stream of words from my mouth. from my
lips, an old river valley. we're
new people in the old tried
land whispering the old tired place-names. and a whisper does
not break this thickening silence.
what did you talk about rolling over and over and under the bed.
like that.
fly sqat.

i did not talk about the wet snail trail i leave on the sheets i
did not say rub against me hot and cold like a bath tap right
there, no
further down.
just right.
i slept with a zip pinned across both lips.
dry and cracked the rainy season stayed inside me.
we use up between one, between the two of us
all our words washing them in the long hot silences.
and the quiet sucks and sneaks purring in every hollow of our
bodies.
it is not soft this oozing.
it is strong hot loud from the storms of many years. there are
no words wide enough to speak this weather. and so we get
wet in damp silence.
for years we close up eyes mouth skin to the live wires
that skip from here to you to here.

and a line of humming and down my body cicadas
buzzing drown our sharp breathing. the pillows bank up
underneath the panting sky
they are grey stormclouds. i
scrape over you dusty dry thirsty

there is no water no running tap
only this drought on words between this this and that mouth

i did not talk about the gush of the thunderstorm that
brews in and between. we talk about small talk
about the weather mostly. the ground cries out
for wet you say. i hedge around
your words the way your arms avoid my legs. i make excuses
for your gasps and rasping, i make excuses.
but i cannot hold back this sudden flood of sweat the
drops of words that form about your lips.
take a long cool drink without swallowing it up again.
take the names of these places on my face that slip away,
there's an inland sea between the sheets.
in the haze of the afternoon
we're breaking the rules breaking the drought.

NOTES

Introduction

1. From an interview in *Mattoid* No 13, ed. Wendy Morgan and Sneja Gunew, Deakin University, Geelong, Vic.
2. These are: *Modern Australian Poetry*, ed. David Campbell, Sun Books, Melbourne, 1970; *Australian Poetry Now*, ed. Tom Shapcott, Sun Books, Melbourne, 1970; *12 Poets 1950-1970*, ed. Alexander Craig, Jacaranda Press, Sydney, 1971; *The Penguin Book of Australian Verse*, ed. H. Heseltine, Penguin, Ringwood, 1972; *The First Paperback Poets Anthology*, ed. Roger McDonald, UQP, St Lucia, 1974; *Applestealers*, ed. R. Kenny and C. Talbot, Outback Press, Melbourne, 1974; *The New Australian Poetry*, ed. John Tranter, Makar, Newcastle, 1979; *The Golden Apples of the Sun*, ed. Chris Wallace-Crabbe, MUP, Melbourne, 1981; *Gargoyle Series* (to No 30), ed. Martin Duwell, Makar, Queensland; *The Penguin Book of Modern Australian Verse*, ed. H. Heseltine, Penguin, Ringwood, 1981; *The Collins Book of Australian Poetry*, ed. Rodney Hall, Collins, Sydney, 1981; *The Second Paperback Poets Anthology*, ed. Tom Shapcott, UQP, St Lucia, 1982; *The Younger Australian Poets*, ed. R. Gray and G. Lehmann, Hale & Iremonger, Sydney, 1983; *The Heritage of Australian Poetry*, ed. Geoffrey Dutton, Currey O'Neil, Melbourne, 1984; *Neither Nuked Nor Crucified*, ed. Christopher Pollnitz, Mattara, Newcastle, 1984.
3. Back cover, *Condition Red*, Vicki Viidikas, UQP, St Lucia, 1973.
4. For an interesting discussion of the language often used to describe women's writing, see *Man Made Language*, Dale Spender, Routledge and Kegan Paul, London, 1980.
5. In 'Questionnaires on poetry', *Australian Literary Studies*, Vol. 8 No. 2, October 1977.
6. *A Gap in the Records*, Jan McKemmish, Sybylla, Melbourne, 1985.
7. In *Quilt*, Finola Moorhead, Sybylla, Melbourne, 1985.
8. From the article 'Dance Floor Clues to a Better Society' in the *Sydney Morning Herald*, 1984.
9. 'The Map of the World' from *The Train* in *Leaving Queensland and The Train*, Barbara Brooks and Anna Couani, Sea Cruise Books, 1983.
10. Statement of poetics in *Off the Record*, an anthology of contemporary performance poems. Compiled and edited by II O, Penguin, 1985.
11. *Ibid*.
12. *Ibid*.
13. *Ibid*.
14. In a review 'Goodbye Prince Hamlet: The New Australian Women's Poetry' in *Quilt*, *op. cit*.
15. The current magazines and journals are available in the serials rooms of university libraries. The feminist ones are also available at Gleebooks and the Feminist Bookshop in Sydney, and Shrew Bookshop and International Bookshop in Melbourne.

e voice-over script of *Desert Stories*, a documentary film by Billy
king.
Tamsin Donaldson of the Australian Institute of Aboriginal Studies
r this point.
in Donaldson's discussion of Aboriginal song texts and translation
boriginal History 3:62-83, 1979.

19. In *Black Reflections*, a report on a Commonwealth Schools Commission project, published by the Education Information Retrieval Service.

20. In his *History of Australian Literature*.

21. What happens to women's writing and the strategies for suppressing it, is well documented in *How to Suppress Women's Writing*, Joanna Russ, The Women's Press, London, 1984.

22. David Garnett in his Introduction to *Selected Poems* by Anna Wickham, Chatto and Windus, London, 1971. Virago Press published *The Writings of Anna Wickham: Free Woman and Poet* (404 pp), ed. and introduced by R. D. Smith in 1984.

23. In 'Poetry and sexual difference: Notes towards an Australian female poetic' in *Meanjin*, March–April, 1985.

24. From the Introduction to *The Best of Ethel Anderson: Tales of Parramatta and India*, edited by John Douglas Pringle, Angus and Robertson, Sydney, 1973.

25. From the Introduction to *The Poems of Lesbia Harford*, ed. Drusilla Modjeska and Marjorie Pizer, Sirius Books, Sydney, 1985. Colleen Burke is also working on editions of early women poets. See her *Doherty's Corner*, the poems of Marie Pitt, Angus and Robertson, Sydney, 1985. A biography and selection of the poems of Mary Fullerton ('E') will be available soon.

26. For an enlightening analysis of contemporary poetry by lesbian women in the USA, see Elly Bulkin's introduction to *Lesbian Poetry*, ed. by Elly Bulkin and Joan Larkin, Persephone Press, Massachusetts, 1981. Bulkin mentions Gertrude Stein and Amy Lowell and H. D as early figures in a lesbian literary tradition; included in the anthology are such poets as May Sarton, Adrienne Rich, Audre Lorde, Judy Grahn (who has won the American Poetry Review Prize), Marilyn Hacker, Susan Griffin, and Rita Mae Brown.

27. From 'Feminists and post-modernism' in *The Anti-Aesthetic, Essays on Postmodern Culture*, ed. Hal Foster, Bay Press, Washington, 1983.

28. From 'Negative capability as practice in women's art' in *Studio International*, 1976, Jan/Feb, Vol. 191 No. 979, page 25. Quoted in *Heartland*, a catalogue of six Australian women artists, for a travelling exhibition assisted by the Visual Arts Board of the Australia Council, 1985.

BIOGRAPHICAL NOTES

ETHEL ANDERSON
Born Leamington, UK, 1883. Lived in India for a long time before coming to Australia. Published six books including *Squatter's Luck and Other Bucolic Eclogues* (Melbourne University Press, 1954). Died 1958.

DOROTHY AUCHTERLONIE
Born Sunderland, England, 1915. Has worked as academic and journalist for many years. First woman lecturer on the staff of Monash University, Melbourne, taught at Duntroon Military Academy, Canberra. *Ulysses Bound*, her analysis of the novels of Henry Handel Richardson (1974) is a landmark in Australian literary criticism. Published *The Dolphin* (ANU Press, 1967), *The Music of Love* (Penguin Books, 1985). Lives in Canberra.

STEFANIE BENNETT
Born Townsville, Queensland, 1945. Published books include *Poems from the Paddywagon* (Cochon, 1973), *The Medium* (Khasmik Enterprises). Lives in Scarborough, Queensland.

JUDITH BEVERIDGE
Born London, 1956. Has a BA in Communications from New South Wales Institute of Technology. Works as a library assistant and teaches creative writing at a technical college. Received a writing grant from the Literature Board in 1985. Her collections of poetry *From the Curved City* to be published soon by Black Lightning Press. Lives in Sydney.

JENNY BOULT
Born Warwickshire, England, 1951. Publications include *The Hotel Anonymous* (Bent Enterprises, 1980), *the white rose and the bath* (Friendly Street Poets, 1984), *Can't Help Dreaming* (All Out Ensemble, 1981). Edited *Pearls: Writing by South Australian Women* (Anthology Collective, 1980) and *After the Rage: South Australian Women's Art and Writing* (with Tess Brady, Tutu Press, 1983). Teaches creative writing and lives in Adelaide.

ANNE BREWSTER
Born Sydney, 1956. Writing her MA thesis on science fiction and teaches at the Western Australian Institute of Technology, Perth.

PAMELA BROWN
Born Seymour, Victoria, 1949. Has published seven books of poetry, including *Selecting Poems* (Redress Press, 1984). Lives in Sydney and works at an art college teaching video production.

COLLEEN BURKE

Born Bondi, New South Wales, 1943. Published *The Incurable Romantic* (Outback Press 1979), *She Moves Mountains* (Redress Press 1984) and *Doherty's Corner*, the poems of Marie Pitt. Currently working on a biography and selection of the poems of Mary Fullerton ('E'). Lives in Sydney and works in community health.

JOANNE BURNS

Born Sydney, 1945. Her books include *Adrenalin Flickknife* (Saturday Centre, 1974), *Ventriloquy* (Sea Cruise Books, 1981), *Alphabetics: Children's Stories on Language* (Saturday Centre, 1985). Works as a teacher and lives in Sydney.

CAROLINE CADDY

Born USA 1944. Published *Singing at Night* (Fremantle Arts Centre Press, 1980), *Letters from the North* (Fremantle Arts Centre Press, 1985). Farms at Denmark, Western Australia.

ADA CAMBRIDGE

Novelist and poet, born 1844. She has been called 'the first Australian writer . . . to whom social problems really mattered'. Died 1926.

LUCINDA CASTALDI

Born Sydney 1961. Majored in writing at New South Wales Institute of Technology. Works at State Library of New South Wales. Lives in Sydney.

LEE CATALDI

Born Sydney 1942. Published *Invitation to a Marxist Lesbian Party* (Wild and Woolley, 1978). Lives on an Aboriginal settlement in the Northern Territory, where she teaches.

NANCY CATO

Born Adelaide, 1917. Novelist and poet. Published *The Darkened Window* (Lyrebird Writers 1950), *The Dancing Bough* (Angus and Robertson, 1957), *All the Rivers Run* (1978).

CHRISTINE CHURCHES

Born Keith, South Australia, 1945. Published *My Mother and the Trees* (Angus and Robertson, 1977). Has won several scholarships to Italy to study antiquities. Lives in Adelaide.

AILEEN CORPUS

Born Darwin 1950 and raised in the Retta Dixon Children's Home. Her tribal name is Ne'eri, of the Wagiman and the Nangumerri peoples of the Northern Territory. Has published in magazines. Works as a community arts officer and lives in Darwin.

ANNA COUANI

Born Sydney 1948. Trained as an architect, now teaches art. Published *Were All Women Sex Mad?*, *Italy*, *Leaving Queensland and the Train* (with Barbara Brooks, 1983). Active in the Poets Union and is the publisher of Sea Cruise Books in Sydney.

ZORA CROSS
Born 1890. Published extensively: *A Song of Mother Love* (1916), *Songs of Love and Life* (Angus and Robertson, 1917), *The Lilt of Life* (Angus and Robertson, 1918), *Elegy of an Australian School Boy* (Angus and Robertson, 1921). Also wrote plays. Died 1964.

SARAH DAY
Born Ormskirk, UK, 1956. Travelled to France on a Literature Board grant in 1985. Lives in Hobart where she teaches tertiary English courses.

ROSEMARY DOBSON
Born Sydney 1920. Has published several books of poetry, including *Child with a Cockatoo and Other Poems* (1948), *Selected Poems* (1973), *Over the Frontier* (1978) and *The Three Fates and Other Poems* (1984). Has edited four anthologies, including *Sisters Poets I* (Sisters Publishing, 1979). Given Robert Frost Award for Poetry 1979. Lives in Canberra.

MARY DURACK
Born Adelaide 1913. Journalist, playwright, novelist, historian, biographer and poet. Awarded OBE and DBE. Lives in Nedlands, Western Australia.

ANNE ELDER
Born New Zealand 1918. Grew up in Melbourne and was a solo dancer with the Borovansky Ballet. Died 1976. Publications include *For the Record* (Hawthorn Press, 1972) and *Crazy Women* (Angus and Robertson, 1976). The Anne Elder Memorial Prize is given for a first book of poetry by an Australian writer.

MARY FINNIN
Born Geelong, Victoria, 1906. Work published by Jindyworobak, the *Bulletin* and *Overland*.

MARY FULLERTON ('E')
Born Glenmaggie, Victoria, 1868. Published four books of poetry. Died 1946.

KATHERINE GALLAGHER
Born Maldon, Victoria, 1935. Started writing poetry in 1965. Published *The Eye's Circle* (Rigmarole, 1975), *Tributaries of the Love Song* (Angus and Robertson, 1978) and *Passengers to the City* (Hale & Iremonger, 1985). Lives in London.

SILVANA GARDNER
Born Zadar, Yugoslavia, 1942. Poet and artist. Published *Hacedor* (Planet Press, 1980), *When Sunday Comes* (UQP, 1982), *With Open Eyes* (Queensland Community Press, 1983). Lives in Brisbane.

BARBARA GILES
Born England 1912. Novelist and poet. Has edited *Luna* magazine, Melbourne. Has published *Eve Rejects Apple* (Angus and Robertson, 1978) and *Earth and Solitude* (Pariah Press, 1984). Lives in Melbourne.

MARY GILMORE

Political activist and writer, born near Goulburn, New South Wales, 1865. Joined the group of Australians led by William Lane who set up a new society in Paraguay in 1902. Widely published in political and literary journals. Created a Dame of the British Empire. Edited the women's pages of the *Worker* for thirty-three years. Died aged ninety-seven in 1962.

ELAINE GOLDING

Born near Birmingham, UK, 1950. Works as teacher and lives in Adelaide.

NANCY GORDON

Born Kensington, Melbourne, 1918. Published *Not Crab but Butterfly* (Raphael Arts, 1977). Lives in Adelaide.

SUSAN HAMPTON

Born Inverell, New South Wales, 1949. Published *Costumes* (Transit Press, 1982) and *About Literature* (with Sue Woolfe; Macmillan, 1984). Teaches writing and theory courses in Sydney and Newcastle.

LESBIA HARFORD

Born Melbourne 1891. Graduated in Arts and Law from University of Melbourne. Worked for political reasons in a clothing factory while being politically active on behalf o' women's rights. Died 1927. *The Poems of Lesbia Harford* edited by Nettie Palmer published 1941 and *Selected Poems* (edited Drusilla Modjeska and Marjorie Pizer) published 1985.

J. S. HARRY

Born Adelaide 1939. Published *the deer under the skin* (UQP, 1971), *Hold, for a little while and turn gently* (Island Press, 1979), *Dandelion for Van Gogh* (Island Press, 1985). Awarded the Harri Jones Memorial Prize 1971. Lives in Sydney.

ISABEL HARTMAN

Born Adelaide 1958. Teaches and lives in Adelaide.

GWEN HARWOOD

Born Brisbane 1920. Has published *Poems* (Angus and Robertson, 1963) and *Poems Volume Two* (Angus and Robertson, 1968), *Selected Poems* (Angus and Robertson, 1975), *The Lion's Bride* (Angus and Robertson, 1981). Won Grace Leven Prize 1975, Robert Frost Award 1977 and Patrick White Award 1977. She is librettest to composer Larry Stisky and lives in Tasmania.

JILL HELLYER

Born Sydney 1925. Biographer and novelist, co-founder of the Australian Society of Authors and first executive officer 1963-71. Published *The Exile* (1969), *Song of the Humpback Whales* (Sisters Publishing, 1981). Lives near Sydney.

DOROTHY HEWETT
Born Perth 1923. Playwright, novelist and poet. Books of poetry include *Windmill Country* (1965), *Rapunzel in Suburbia* (1979), *Greenhouse* (1979). Plays include *Chapel Perilous* (1971), *This Old Man Comes Rolling Home* (1976), *The Man from Mukinupin* (1980), *Golden Oldies* (1981), *Susannah's Dreaming* (1981), and *The Fields of Heaven* (1982). Lives in Sydney.

OLIVE HOPEGOOD
Born (?) 1900. Work published by *Meanjin* and Jindyworobak.

WENDY JENKINS
Born Perth 1952. Published *Out of Water Into Light* (Fremantle Arts Centre Press, 1979). Member of Literature Board of the Australia Council. Works in publishing. Lives in Western Australia.

KATE JENNINGS
Born New South Wales 1949. Edited *Mother I'm Rooted* (Outback Press, 1975), an anthology that had an enormous effect on Australia's women poets. Published *Come to Me, My Melancholy Baby* (Outback Press, 1975). Lives and works as an editor in New York.

ELIZABETH JOLLEY
Born Birmingham, UK, 1923. Arrived in Australia in 1959. She has had stories, plays and poems published in Australian literary journals and anthologies, and broadcast on British and Australian radio. Acclaimed as one of Australia's leading fiction writers, she won the *Age* Book of the Year award for *Mr Scobie's Riddle*. Lives in Western Australia.

BEATE JOSEPHI
Born Trier, West Germany, 1948. PhD University of Wiesbaden. Works as radio journalist and critic. Chairperson 1986 Writers' Week Committee of Adelaide Festival of Arts. Lives in Adelaide.

SYLVIA KANTARIS
Born Derbyshire, UK, 1936. Lived in Australia from 1962 to 1973. Published *Time and Motion* (Prism Books, 1975), *News from the Front* (with D. M. Thomas, Harry Chambers/Peterloo Poets, 1983), *The Tenth Muse* (Harry Chambers/Peterloo Poets, 1983), *The Sea at the Door* (Secker and Warburg, 1985).

NANCY KEESING
Born Sydney 1923. Many publications, including two novels for children, criticism, biography. Poetry books include *Immanent* (Lyrebird Writers, 1951), *Three Men of Sydney* (Angus and Robertson, 1955), *Hails and Farewells* (Edwards and Shaw, 1977). Edited *Australian Bush Ballads* with Douglas Stewart (Angus and Robertson, 1955). Member of Literature Board and later Chairperson, Member of Order of Australia.

ANTIGONE KEFALA

Born Braila, Rumania, 1934. Published *The Alien* (Makar Press, 1973), *Thirsty Weather* (Outback press, 1978), two short novels under title *The First Journey* (1975). Works as arts administrator with the Australia Council, lives in Sydney.

JEAN KENT

Born Chinchilla, Queensland, 1951. Works as psychologist. Lives Kilaben Bay, New South Wales.

JERI KROLL

Born New York City, USA, 1946. Published *Death as Mr Right* (Friendly Street Poets, 1982), *Indian Movies* (Hyland House, 1984). PhD Columbia University. Teaches and lives in Adelaide.

NORA KROUK

Born Harbin, China, 1920. She matriculated in Russian and has studied a number of foreign languages. Worked as a journalist in Hong Kong. Published *Even Though* (Hong Kong, 1975). Now lives in Sydney, and works as a translator.

EVE LANGLEY

Born Forbes, New South Wales, 1908. Wrote a number of novels, including *The Peapickers* (1942) and *White Topee* (1954). She believed she was a reincarnation of Oscar Wilde. Lived as a recluse in the bush near Katoomba for some years. Died 1974.

JOYCE LEE

Born Wimmera, Victoria, 1913. Worked as pharmacist for thirty-five years. Poetry published by Sisters Publishing, 1979, and *Abruptly from the Flatlands* (Pariah Press, 1984). Lives in Melbourne.

KATE LILLEY

Born Perth 1960. Awarded three-year research scholarship to Oxford University to write a book on seventeenth-century women poets.

KATE LLEWELLYN

Born Tumby Bay, South Australia, 1940. Published *Trader Kate and the Elephants* (Friendly Street Poets, 1982), *Luxury* (Redress Press, 1985). Joint winner of the Anne Elder Prize. Lives in Leura, New South Wales.

ANNE LLOYD

Born Manly, New South Wales, 1954. Published *The Hips Slither* (Black Lightning Press, 1982). Lecturer in journalism at Rockhampton, Queensland.

DOROTHEA MACKELLAR

Born Sydney 1885. Famous for poem 'My Country'; her other work is much less well known. Died 1968. *The Poems of Dorothea Mackellar* was published by Rigby Ltd. 1971.

RHYLL McMASTER
Born Brisbane 1947. Published *The Brineshrimp* (UQP, 1972), *Washing the Money* (Angus and Robertson, 1986). Farms outside Canberra.

JENNIFER MAIDEN
Born Penrith, New South Wales, 1949. Has published *Tactics* (UQP, 1974), *Mortal Details* (Rigmarole Press), *The Problem of Evil* (Prism Books, 1975), *Birth Stones* (Angus and Robertson, 1982), *The Border Loss* (Angus and Robertson), *For the Left Hand* (Poetry Australia), *The Terms* (a novel, Hale and Iremonger). Has taught over one thousand creative writing classes in Sydney's western suburbs. Lives in Penrith.

CHRIS MANSELL
Born Sydney 1953. Published *Delta* (1978), *Head Heart & Stone* (Fling Books, 1982). Editor of *Compass* magazine. Lives in Sydney.

ANNA MUNSTER
Born Sydney 1963. Studied philosophy and feminism at Sydney University. Coedited *Come 2*, a cassette magazine for women. Works in the area of experimental sound. Lives in Sydney.

VERA NEWSOM
Born Manchester, UK, 1912. Educated in Auckland and then at Sydney University. Published in many literary magazines, newspapers and anthologies. Teaches poetry workshops and writes critical reviews. Has completed a book of poems, *Tapestry*. Lives in Sydney.

ROSEMARY NISSEN
Born Launceston, Tasmania, 1939. Co-edited *Dictionary of Australian Poets* (1980). Published *Universe Cat* (Abalone Press, 1984). Lives in Melbourne. Works as a librarian and creative writing teacher in prisons.

CAROL NOVACK
Born New York City, USA, 1948. Published *Living Alone Without a Dictionary* (Makar Press,1974), has work in *Island in the Sun* (Sea Cruise Books, 1980).

THUY AI NGUYEN THI
Born Quang Nam, Vietnam, in 1947. Won poetry prizes at high school and at the University of Saigon, where she studied law. Came to Australia in 1982 as a refugee. A member of the Huong Viet Pen Group, her poems are published in Vietnamese magazines and newspapers. Lives in Sydney.

JAN OWEN
Born Adelaide 1940. Published *Boy With Telescope* (Angus and Robertson, 1986). Lives in Surrey Downs, South Australia.

CHARMAINE PAPERTALK-GREEN

Born Eradu, via Geraldton, Western Australia. Currently a student in Canberra and works at the Australian Institute of Aboriginal Affairs. Lives in Canberra.

GRACE PERRY

Born Melbourne 1927. Works as medical practitioner in Berrima, New South Wales. Has published six books of poetry and edited *Poetry Australia* for many years.

DOROTHY PORTER

Born Sydney 1954. Published *Little Hoodlum* (Prism Books, 1975), *Bison* (Prism Books, 1979), *The Night Parrot* (Black Lightning Press, 1984). Lives in Sydney where she teaches creative writing courses in prisons and technical colleges.

JENNIFER RANKIN

Born Sydney, 1941. Published *Ritual Shift* (Makar Press, 1975) and *Earth Hold* (Secker & Warburg, 1978). Widely published in Australia and the United Kingdom. Died 1979.

RICKETTY KATE (MINNIE AGNES FILSON)

Born (?) 1900. Published under name of Ricketty Kate because she was handicapped with arthritis. Published *Out of the Dust* (undated) herself.

ELIZABETH RIDDELL

Born Napier, New Zealand, 1910. Journalist and poet who has travelled and written extensively. Published *Forbears* (Angus and Robertson, 1961) and *Poems* (Ure Smith). Lives in Sydney.

LARAINE ROCHE

Born 1948. Published *Child on the Rocks* (Khasmik Enterprises, 1975).

JUDITH RODRIGUEZ

Born Perth 1936. Poet and woodcut artist. Was poetry editor of *Meanjin* 1979-82, is reviewer for *Sydney Morning Herald*. Published *A Question of Ignorance* (Cheshire, 1962), *Nu-Plastik Fanfare Red* (University of Queensland Press, 1973), *Water Life* (UQP, 1976), *Shadow on Glass* (Open Door Press, 1978), *Mudcrab at Gambaros* (UQP, 1980), *Witch Heart* (Sisters Publishing, 1982), edited *Mrs Noah and the Minoan Queen* (Sisters Publishing, 1983). Lives in Sydney.

GIG RYAN

Born Melborne 1956. Published *The Division of Anger* (Transit Poetry, 1982) and *Manners of an Astronaut* (Hale and Iremonger, 1985). Widely published in magazines. Poet, guitarist and singer. Lives in Sydney.

DIPTI SARAVANAMUTTU

Born Sri Lanka 1960. Graduated from the University of Sydney and travelled in Asia. Poems published in many magazines. Lives and works in Sydney.

MARGARET SCOTT
Born Bristol, UK, 1934. Has published two books of poetry and has had work published in *Island* magazine. Lecturer at University of Hobart, Tasmania.

ALEXANDRA SEDDON
Born London 1944. Published *Full Circle* (1970), *Sparrows* (Carcanet Press, 1970), *Green Feet* (Glandular Press, 1981). Lives on a farm at Candels, New South Wales.

EDITH SPEERS
Born Canada, 1949. Arrived in Australia 1974. Has been published in various literary magazines here and overseas. Trained as a biochemist. Now lives on a farm in southern Tasmania and is writing a book on astrology.

MADGE STAUNTON
Born Coolangatta, Queensland, 1917. Painter and poet. Published *The Cleaving Wedge* (Queensland Community Press, 1982). Died 1986.

AMANDA STEWART
Born London 1959. Grew up in Sydney. Works at the ABC in Sydney. Involved in performance and sound poetry.

JENNIFER STRAUSS
Born Heywood, Victoria, 1933. Has published *Children and Other Strangers* (Nelson, 1975), *Winter Driving* (Sisters Publishing, 1981). Currently lecturer in Department of English, Monash University, Victoria.

BOBBI SYKES
Born Townsville, Queensland, 1945. Aboriginal political activist who works as freelance consultant on social issues. Has published *Love Poems and Other Revolutionary Acts* (Saturday Centre). Harvard graduate with Doctorate of Education. Lives in Sydney.

JEAN TALBOT
Born Hull, UK, 1937. Widely published and anthologised in Hunter Valley publications. Lives in New Lambton, New South Wales.

thalia
Born Greece 1952. Migrated to Australia 1954. Co-editor *925*, a poetry magazine about work. Lives and works in Melbourne.

VICKI VIIDIKAS
Born Sydney 1948, has travelled widely in India. Has published *Condition Red* (UQP, 1973), *Wrappings* (Wild and Woolley, 1974), *Knabel* (Wild and Woolley, 1978), *India Ink* (Hale and Iremonger, 1984).

ANIA WALWICZ
Born Swidnica Slaska, Poland, 1951. Works in the visual and performing arts as well as poetry. Published *Writing* (Rigmarole Books, 1979). Work included in *Island in the Sun* (Sea Cruise Books, 1981). Lives in Melbourne.

KATH WALKER
Born Brisbane 1920. Black political activist who says, 'I am of the Noonuccal tribe of Stradbroke Island, near Brisbane, my totem the carpet snake.' Published *We Are Going* (Jacaranda Press, 1964), *The Dawn is at Hand* (Jacaranda Press, 1966), *My People* (Jacaranda Press, 1970), *Stradbroke Dreamtime* (Angus and Robertson, 1972).

ANNA WICKHAM
Born Wimbledon, UK, 1884. Grew up in Australia and returned to Europe at the age of twenty to study singing. Knew many luminaries of the period such as Epstein, Frieda and D. H. Lawrence and Augustus John. Died 1947. Virago Books published a collection of her works in 1985.

JUDITH WRIGHT
Born Armidale, New South Wales, 1915. Conservationist also involved in the Aboriginal land rights movement. She has published eleven books of poetry, a family history *Generations of Men* (1959), and *Cry for the Dead* (1981). Published also *Collected Poems* (Angus and Robertson, 1971), edited anthology *A Book of Australian Verse* (Oxford University Press, 1956). Lives Moongalbie, New South Wales.

FAY ZWICKY
Born Melbourne 1933. Concert pianist, critic, poet, editor and short story writer. Books of poetry include *Isaac Babel's Fiddle* (1975), *Kaddish and Other Poems* (1982), has edited *Quarry* (1981) and *Journeys* (1982). Has travelled widely and lived in Indonesia, America and Europe. At present a lecturer in the Department of English, University of Western Australia.

INDEX OF FIRST LINES

INDEX OF AUTHORS

ACKNOWLEDGEMENTS

For permission to reprint the poems in this anthology, acknowledgement is made to the following:

Aboriginal Songs: collected and translated by Catherine Berndt, from her 'Expressions of Grief Among Aboriginal Women' in *Oceania*, Vol. XX, no. 4, 1950.

Ethel Anderson: 'Three Satires', from *Squatter's Luck*, to Melbourne University Press.

Anonymous: 'The Female Transport', from *Old Bush Songs and Rhymes of Colonial Times*, edited by Douglas Stewart, Angus & Robertson, 1957.

Dorothy Auchterlonie: 'A Problem of Language' and 'Present Tense', from *The Dolphin*, ANU Press, to the author.

Stefanie Bennett: 'Union Jacks', from *The Medium*, Khasmik Enterprises, to the author.

Judith Beveridge: 'The Domesticity of Giraffes', 'Making Perfume', 'Streets of Chippendale' and 'My Name', to the author.

Jenny Boult: 'admiring the handiwork', from *the white rose and the bath*, Friendly Street Poets, to the author.

Anne Brewster: 'Ghoul' from *Friendly Street Reader No. 6*, Friendly Street Poets, to the author.

Pamela Brown: 'One for Patti Smith', The Red Cocacola Bottle', 'Honky Tonk Sunset', 'who is this guy', 'the longer I write poems for you', 'Leaving' and 'The Dear John Letter' from *Selected Poems*, Redress Press/Wild & Woolley, to the author.

Colleen Burke: 'Why we didn't go away on the weekend', 'Call Around and See Us' and 'I Feel Lousy', from *The Incurable Romantic* (1979), Outback Press, to the author.

Joanne Burns: 'real land' from *Ventriloquy*, 'stacking it/another suicide' from *Adrenalin Flicknife*, 'she had more friends' from *Ratz* and 'Pillow' from *Compass*, to the author.

Caroline Caddy: 'Lenny' from *Letters from the North* (1985) Fremantle Arts Centre Press, to the author.

Ada Cambridge: 'Desire' and 'Vows' from *The Hand in the Dark and Other Poems* (1913), Heinemann UK, out of copyright.

Lucinda Castaldi: 'The Dummies', to the author.

Lee Cataldi: 'Evening and All That Jazz', from *Invitation to a Marxist Lesbian Party*, Wild & Woolley, to the author.

Nancy Cato: 'Mallee Farmer' and 'Day's End', from *The Dancing Bough*, to Angus & Robertson.

Christine Churches: 'My Mother and the Trees', from *Poets of the Month, Series 3*, to Angus & Robertson.

Aileen Corpus: 'blkfern-jungal' and 'Taxi Conversation', to the author.

Anna Couani: 'The Train' and 'The Map of the World' from *Leaving Queensland and The Train*, Sea Cruise Books; 'Drawing the Fruit', 'What a man, what a moon' and 'We could smell the salt', to the author.

Zora Cross: 'Thou Shalt Not' and 'Love Sonnets' from *Songs of Love and Life*, to Angus & Robertson.

Sarah Day: 'Greenhouse Tomatoes', to the author.

Rosemary Dobson: 'Good Friday, Boston' and 'The Nightmare' from *The Three Fates* (1984), Hale and Iremonger, to Curtis Brown (Aust) Ltd; 'Child with a Cockatoo' and 'Captain Svenson', from *Rosemary Dobson: Selected Poems*, to Angus & Robertson; 'The Eye', to Curtis Brown (Aust) Ltd.

Mary Durack: 'Lament for the Drowned Country', to the author.

Anne Elder: 'Crazy Woman' and 'Seen Out' from *Crazy Woman*, to Angus & Robertson.

Mary Finnin: 'Breaking Drought', to the author.

Mary Fullerton ('E'): 'Gadgets', 'Puppets', 'Threads', 'Lion' and 'Humility', to Angus & Robertson.

Katherine Gallagher: 'Passengers to the City' and 'Concerning Native Fauna', to the author.

Silvana Gardner: 'Shadow Ape', from *With Open Eyes*, Queensland Community Press, to the author.

Barbara Giles: 'Fireworks and Champagne' and 'Learning All the Words in the World', from *Earth and Solitude* (1984), Pariah Press, to the author.

Mary Gilmore: 'What?', from scrapbook of her writings, Mitchell Library; 'The Woman', 'Awakened', 'The Kiss', 'Marri'd', 'Honing up the Hill' and 'Old Botany Bay' from *The Passionate Heart and Other Poems*, to Angus & Robertson.

Elaine Golding: 'Genesis/take 2', from *Friendly Street Reader No. 6*, Friendly Street Poets, to the author.

Nancy Gordon: 'The Night She Explored Her Psyche', from *Friendly Street Poets No. 5*, to the author.

Susan Hampton: 'Yugoslav Story', from *Costumes*, Transit Press, to the author; 'Stranded in Paradise' and 'Statues', to the author.

Lesbia Harford: 'Untitled — 24/7/18' from *The Poems of Lesbia Harford* to Melbourne University Press.

J. S. Harry: 'the gulf of bothnia', from *A Dandelion for Van Gogh*, Island Press, to the author; 'the poem films itself', from *hold, for a little while, and turn gently*, Island Press, to the author; 'subjective around lismore' and 'uncle with currawongs', to the author.

Isabel Hartman: 'Check Mate', to the author.

Gwen Harwood: 'An Address to My Muse', from *The Lion's Bride*, to Angus & Robertson; 'Night Thoughts: Baby & Demon', 'I am the Captain of my Soul',

'Carnal Knowledge II' and 'Suburban Sonnet: Boxing Day', from *Gwen Harwood: Selected Poems*, to Angus & Robertson; 'Mid-Channel', to the author.

Jill Hellyer: 'Jonah's Wife', from *Song of the Humpback Whales*, Sisters Publishing Ltd, to the author.

Dorothy Hewett: 'This Time' and 'Anniversary' from *Rapunzel in Suburbia* (1975), Prism/New Poetry, to the author; 'Fourth Exile's Letter', from *Greenhouse*, Big Smoke Books, to the author.

Wendy Jenkins: 'Against Noise', to the author.

Kate Jennings: 'Couples' and 'One Kiss Too Many', from *Come to Me My Melancholy Baby* (1975), Outback Press, to the author.

Elizabeth Jolley: 'Neighbour Woman on the Fencing Wire', from *Quarry* (1981), Fremantle Arts Centre Press, to the author.

Beate Josephi: 'Tuscan Dream', from *Friendly Street Reader No. 8*, Friendly Street Poets, to the author.

Sylvia Kantaris: 'The Tenth Muse', 'Package for the Distant Future' and 'Annunciation', from *The Tenth Muse* (1983), Peterloo Poets, to the author; 'Travelogue', from *The Sea at the Door* (1985), Secker & Warburg, to the poet; 'News From the Front', from *News From the Front* (1983), co-author D. M. Thomas, Arc Publications, to the poet.

Nancy Keesing: 'The Three Ring Circus', from *Lines from the Horizon* (1982), University of Newcastle, to the author; 'Female Spider-Spider Female', from *Hails and Farewells* (1977), Edwards & Shaw, to the author.

Antigone Kefala: 'Freedom Fighter', from *Mrs Noah and the Minoan Queen* (1983), Sisters Publishing Ltd, to the author.

Jean Kent: 'To the Ironingboard', to the author.

Jeri Kroll: 'Towers of Silence' and 'Bushfire Weather', to the author.

Nora Krouk: Untitled, to the author.

Eve Langley: 'Native-born', from the *Bulletin*.

Joyce Lee: 'Miriol' and 'Dreams for Wheat', from *Abruptly from the Flatlands* (1984), Pariah Press, to the author.

Kate Lilley: 'A Flash of Green' and 'Fabula', to the author.

Kate Llewellyn: 'O', 'The Kites', 'Breasts' and 'Eve' from *Luxury*, Redress Press, to the author.

Anne Lloyd: 'Juds Park', from *The Hips Slither*, Black Lightning Press, to the author.

Dorothea Mackellar: 'Two Japanese Songs', 'Arms and the Woman' and 'My Country', from *The Closed Door*, Rigby, to Curtis Brown (Aust) Pty Ltd.

Rhyll McMaster: 'A festive poem', from *The Brineshrimp* (1972), University of Queensland Press, to the author.

Jennifer Maiden: 'The Trust', to the author.

Chris Mansell: 'Definition Poem: Pissed as a Parrot', from *Head, Heart and Stone*, Fling Poets; 'Lady Gedanke Writes to the Painter' and 'Dialogue', to the author.

Anna Munster: 'breaking the drought', to the author.

Vera Newsom: 'Bricks', to the author.

Rosemary Nissen: 'The Day We Lost the Volkswagen', from *Universe Cat*, to the author.

Carol Novack: 'You try to get out of the fear', from *Living Alone Without a Dictionary* (1974), Makar Press, to the author; 'The Staircase', from *Island in the Sun*, Sea Cruise Books, to the author.

Thuy Ai Nguyen Thi: 'The Quôc Bird', to the author.

Jan Owen: 'Swimming Instructor' and 'Ice-Oh', to the author.

Charmaine Papertalk-Green: 'Wanna be White', to the author.

Grace Perry: 'Waiting for the birth', to the author.

Dorothy Porter: 'The Nashville Poems' and 'The Red Sports Car Afternoon', to the author; 'Scenes From a Marriage' and 'Trial Separation', from *The Night Parrot* (1984), Black Lightning Press, to the author.

Jennifer Rankin: 'I Had A Room', from *Earth Hold* (1978), Secker & Warburg, to David Rankin.

Elizabeth Riddell: 'Occasions of Birds' and 'Kauri' from *Overland*, to the author; 'Personal Notices', to the author.

Judith Rodriguez: 'How do you know it's the right one?', from *Witch Heart* (1982), Sisters Publishing Ltd, to the author; 'The letter from America', to the author; 'Eskimo Occasion', from *Mudcrab at Gambaro's*, 'The Mudcrab-Eaters' and 'black and white, mostly white', from *Nu-Plastik Fanfare Red*, 'Bivalve' and 'Towards Fog', from *Water Life*, all to University of Queensland Press.

Gig Ryan: 'If I Had a Gun', 'Not Like a Wife' and 'Cruising' from *The Division of Anger* (1980), Transit Press, to the author; 'His Cubist Drawings', to the author.

Dipti Saravanamuttu: 'Statistic for the New World', to the author.

Margaret Scott: 'Grandchild' and 'The Black Swans', to the author.

Alexandra Seddon: 'Mornings:3', from *Greenfeet* (1981), Glandular Press, to the author.

Edith Speers: 'Why I Like Men', to the author.

Madge Staunton: 'Writers and War' from *The Cleaving Wedge* (1982), Queensland Community Press, to the estate of Madge Staunton.

Amanda Stewart: 'romance' and 'It becomes: July 1981', to the author.

Jennifer Strauss: 'Guenevere Dying', from *Winter Driving* (1981), Sisters Publishing Ltd, to the author.

Bobbi Sykes: 'Black Woman' and 'Love Poems', from *Love Poems and Other Revolutionary Actions*, Saturday Centre Press, to the author.

Jean Talbot: 'Muse', from *Hunter Valley Poets* (1978), Nimrod Publications, to the author.

thalia: 'Scene', to the author.

Vicki Viidikas: 'Inside of Paradise', 'A Trunkful of Structures', 'It's Natural' and 'Going Down', from *Condition Red* (1973), to University of Queensland Press; 'Rehabilitation', from *Knabel* (1978), Wild & Woolley, to the author.

Ania Walwicz: 'Daredevil', 'Little Red Riding Hood' and 'Marcel Proust', from *Writing* (1979), Rigmarole Books, to the author; 'Australia', from *Island in the*

Sun (1981), Sea Cruise Books, to the author; 'modern ballroom dancing' and 'Leaving', to the author.

Kath Walker: 'No More Boomerang', 'Gifts', 'We are Going' and 'Ballad of the Totems', from *My People*, to Jacaranda Wiley.

Anna Wickham: 'The Sick Assailant', 'Note on Rhyme', 'The Fired Pot' and 'The Marriage', from *The Writings of Anna Wickham: Free Woman and Poet*, to Virago Press, UK.

Judith Wright: 'At a Poetry Conference, Expo '67', 'Stillborn', 'Letter', 'Report of a Working-Party', 'The Trap', 'Eve to Her Daughters' and 'Halfway', from *Collected Poems 1942-1970*, to Angus & Robertson.

Fay Zwicky: 'Mrs Noah Speaks' and 'The Poet Puts It Away', from *Kaddish and Other Poems*, (1982), to University of Queensland Press.

Every effort has been made to trace copyright holders, but in a few cases this has proved impossible. The publishers would be interested to hear from any copyright holders not here acknowledged.